2004 | General

[BLANK PAGE]

G

2640/402

NATIONAL
QUALIFICATIONS
2004

MONDAY, 24 MAY
10.20 AM–11.50 AM

MODERN STUDIES
STANDARD GRADE
General Level

1 Read every question carefully.

2 Answer all questions as fully as you can.

3 If you cannot do a question, go on to the next one. Try again later.

4 In question 3, answer **one** section only; Section (A) The USA or Section (B) Russia or Section (C) China.

5 Write your answers in the answer book provided. Indicate clearly, in the left hand margin, the question and section of question being answered. Do not write in the right hand margin.

SCOTTISH
QUALIFICATIONS
AUTHORITY

SYLLABUS AREA 1—LIVING IN A DEMOCRACY

QUESTION 1

(a)

> *Trade union members can support their union during a dispute.*

Describe **two** actions which *trade union members can take to support their union during a dispute*.

(Knowledge and Understanding, **4** marks)

(b) Study Sources 1 and 2 below, then answer the question which follows.

SOURCE 1

Information about Glenmarsh Textile Factory

Glenmarsh textile factory has lost orders from all over the world. The management wants to cut hours and pay, and to introduce retraining schemes for the workers. The Shop Steward has resigned. Negotiations with the workers are about to start. The new Shop Steward will also have to discuss safety concerns after an accident at the factory and a complaint by two female workers that they have been treated unfairly.

SOURCE 2

Sheila Cameron

Sheila is 55 years old and has worked at Glenmarsh for 12 years. In 1999, she completed a Health and Safety course at union headquarters. She wants to protect the jobs and pay of the workers. In previous disputes she has been a good negotiator. She is very popular with the workers.

Davie Paterson

Davie Paterson is regarded as an expert in dealing with sex discrimination cases. He also has experience of retraining schemes and spoke to the TUC conference about ways to introduce these to companies. He is 54 years old and has worked at Glenmarsh for 10 years.

Using only the information in Sources 1 and 2 above, **explain which person would be the better choice as the Shop Steward** for the workers at Glenmarsh Textiles.

Give **two** reasons for your choice.

You **must** link the information in Source 1 to the person you have chosen.

(Enquiry Skills, **4** marks)

QUESTION 1 (CONTINUED)

(c)

> MSPs work on behalf of the people they represent.

Describe **one** way in which MSPs find out about problems in their local area.

AND

Describe **one** thing the MSP could do to draw attention to problems in his/her local area.

(Knowledge and Understanding, **4** marks)

(d)   Study the information below, then answer the question which follows.

Support for Selected Political Parties in Opinion Polls			
	Conservative	*Labour*	*Liberal Democrat*
2000	34%	44%	17%
2001	30%	46%	17%
2002	32%	41%	21%

Source: ICM Polls

Write down **two** conclusions about support for political parties in the Opinion Polls shown.

You must only use the information above.

(Enquiry Skills, **4** marks)

[Turn over

SYLLABUS AREA 2—CHANGING SOCIETY

QUESTION 2

(a)

> *The Government tries to help unemployed people find work.*

Describe **two** ways in which *the Government tries to help unemployed people find work.*

(Knowledge and Understanding, **4** marks)

(b)

> *Some people need to receive benefits from the government.*

Apart from unemployment, give **two** reasons why *some people need to receive benefits from the government.*

(Knowledge and Understanding, **4** marks)

(c) Study Sources 1 and 2 below and opposite, then answer the question which follows.

SOURCE 1

UK Female Unemployment Rates 1990–2000 (Selected Groups)		
	1990	*2000*
White	6%	5%
Indian	11%	9%
Pakistani/Bangladeshi	25%	21%
African/Caribbean	10%	14%

QUESTION 2 (*c*) (CONTINUED)

SOURCE 2

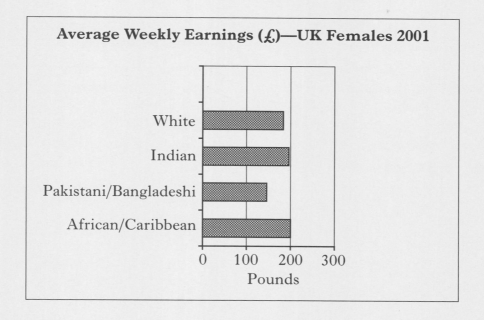

Average Weekly Earnings (£)—UK Females 2001

Pounds

Statements by Sandeep Kholi

- In 2001, white women earned more than all the other female groups.

- The unemployment rate for Indian women fell between 1990 and 2000.

- In 2001, African/Caribbean women earned more than Pakistani/Bangladeshi women.

- All women have similar rates of unemployment.

Using **only** Sources 1 and 2 above, write down **two** statements made by Sandeep Kholi that are **exaggerated**.

Using the statistics in the Sources, give **one** reason why **each** of the statements you have chosen is **exaggerated**.

(Enquiry Skills, **4** marks)

[Turn over

QUESTION 2 (CONTINUED)

(*d*)   Study Sources 1 and 2 below, then answer the question which follows.

SOURCE 1   **SOURCE 2**

View of Government Spokesperson	**View of Opposition Spokesperson**
Free personal and nursing care for the elderly has been available in Scotland since 2002. It has been a great success. Over 75 000 older people have benefited from the extra £150 million we have spent each year. People have a right to health care and the Government should pay for this. Our elderly people expect the best treatment and this is what we will give them.	People should be encouraged to take out private medical insurance and not leave it all to the Government. There are over 10 million elderly people in Britain and this number is growing steadily. The present Government has spent many millions of pounds on a new scheme to provide free personal and nursing care, but this has not worked well.

Sources 1 and 2 give **different** views about **health care for elderly people**.

Write down **two** differences between these views.

You must use only information from the Sources above.

(Enquiry Skills, **4** marks)

SYLLABUS AREA 3—IDEOLOGIES

QUESTION 3

Answer **ONE** section only: Section (A)—The USA on pages seven and eight

        OR Section (B)—Russia on pages nine and ten

        OR Section (C)—China on pages eleven and twelve

(A) THE USA

(a)

Education	Housing	Health

Choose **one** of the topics from the box above.

Give **two** reasons why some members of **ethnic minority groups** often do less well than white Americans in the topic you have chosen.

In your answer, you must refer to ethnic minority groups in the USA that you have studied.

*(Knowledge & Understanding, **4** marks)*

(b) Study Sources 1 and 2 below, then answer the question which follows.

SOURCE 1

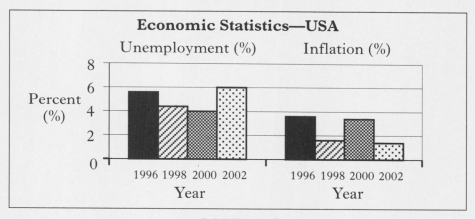

SOURCE 2

Newspaper Report—Industry in the USA

Industrial production in the USA has fallen for the first time in eight years. The terrorist attacks of September 11th 2001 have caused many problems. These have affected American business badly and put industry under great pressure.

The import of cheap goods from other countries like China is also a problem. People are buying imported clothing and electrical goods instead of products made in the USA. These problems have caused share prices to fall.

Unemployment is an increasing problem in the USA. American industry has suffered due to competition from abroad.

                                View of a Democrat Senator

Using **only** Sources 1 and 2 above, give **two** reasons to **support** the view of the Democrat Senator.

Your answer must be based entirely on the sources above.

*(Enquiry Skills, **4** marks)*

QUESTION 3 (A) (CONTINUED)

You are investigating the topic in the box below.

> **The work of the President of the USA**

Answer questions (*c*), (*d*) and (*e*) which follow.

(*c*)   As part of the **planning stage** of your investigation, give **two** relevant aims for your investigation.

(Enquiry Skills, **2** marks)

(*d*)   You decide to use the **Internet** to gather information about **the work of the President of the USA**.

Give **two** ways in which you could use the Internet to help with your investigation.

(Enquiry Skills, **2** marks)

You also decide to use a **library** as a source for your investigation.

(*e*)   Describe **one** advantage and **one** disadvantage of using a library as a source to find out about **the work of the President of the USA**.

(Enquiry Skills, **4** marks)

NOW GO TO QUESTION 4 ON PAGE THIRTEEN

QUESTION 3 (CONTINUED)

(B) RUSSIA

(a)

Education	Housing	Health

Choose **one** of the topics from the box above.

Give **two** reasons why some Russians are better off than others in the topic you have chosen.

(Knowledge & Understanding, **4** marks)

(b) Study Sources 1 and 2 below, then answer the question which follows.

SOURCE 1

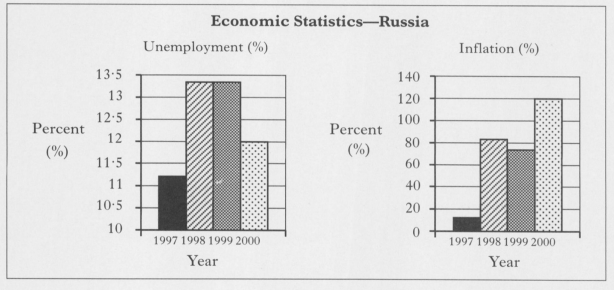

Economic Statistics—Russia

SOURCE 2

Newspaper Report—Industry in Russia

Russian industry has suffered from a lack of investment over the past twenty years. This means that the methods of production are now out-of-date by world standards. Russian industry tends to rely on large numbers of workers. New technology is not as common as in other parts of the world.

Costs of production are high. Because of this, Russia has not been able to attract foreign companies to use the country as a manufacturing centre.

Inflation is an increasing problem in Russia. Russian industry is "old fashioned" compared to the rest of the world.

View of a Communist Deputy

Using **only** Sources 1 and 2 above, give **two** reasons to **support** the view of the Communist Deputy.

(Enquiry Skills, **4** marks)

QUESTION 3 (B) (CONTINUED)

You are investigating the topic in the box below.

The work of the President of Russia

Answer questions (*c*), (*d*) and (*e*) which follow.

(*c*)   As part of the **planning stage** of your investigation, give **two** relevant aims for your investigation.

(Enquiry Skills, **2** marks)

(*d*)   You decide to use the **Internet** to gather information about **the work of the President of Russia**.

Give **two** ways in which you could use the Internet to help with your investigation.

(Enquiry Skills, **2** marks)

You also decide to use a **library** as a source for your investigation.

(*e*)   Describe **one** advantage and **one** disadvantage of using a library as a source to find out about **the work of the President of Russia**.

(Enquiry Skills, **4** marks)

NOW GO ON TO QUESTION 4 ON PAGE THIRTEEN

QUESTION 3 (CONTINUED)

(C) CHINA

(a)

Education	Housing	Health

Choose **one** of the topics from the box above.

Give **two** reasons why some Chinese people are better off than others in the topic you have chosen.

(Knowledge & Understanding, **4** marks)

(b) Study Sources 1 and 2 below, then answer the question which follows.

SOURCE 1

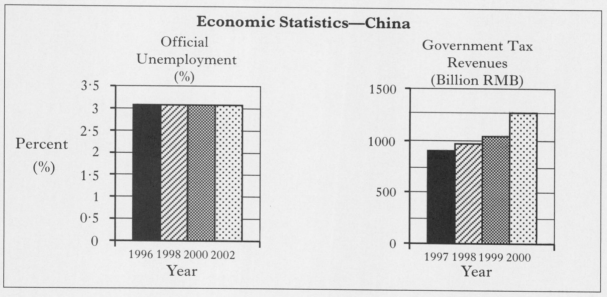

Economic Statistics—China

(c)

SOURCE 2

Newspaper Report—Industry in China

Much of Chinese industry is still state-owned. However, a more competitive market has been introduced meaning that factories must be efficient and make good use of resources. Many Chinese industries now act as a manufacturing centre for foreign countries—China's low wage costs and cheaper production make it attractive.

The links between Chinese industry and the prison camp system are controversial. Some factories use convicted prisoners as their labour force.

Official unemployment rates in China show little change over the years. Chinese industry has benefited from contact with the outside world.

View of a Communist Deputy

Using **only** Sources 1 and 2 above, give **two** reasons to **support** the view of the Communist Deputy.

Your answer must be based entirely on the sources above.

(Enquiry Skills, **4** marks)

QUESTION 3 (C) (CONTINUED)

You are investigating the topic in the box below.

> **The work of the Chinese Communist Party**

Answer questions (*c*), (*d*) and (*e*) which follow.

(*c*) As part of the **planning stage** of your investigation, give **two** relevant aims for your investigation.

(Enquiry Skills, **2** marks)

(*d*) You decide to use the Internet to gather information about **the work of the Chinese Communist Party**.

Give **two** ways in which you could use the Internet to help with your investigation.

(Enquiry Skills, **2** marks)

You also decide to use a **library** as a source for your investigation.

(*e*) Describe **one** advantage and **one** disadvantage of using a library as a source to find out about **the work of the Chinese Communist Party**.

(Enquiry Skills, **4** marks)

NOW GO ON TO QUESTION 4 ON PAGE THIRTEEN

SYLLABUS AREA 4—INTERNATIONAL RELATIONS

QUESTION 4

(a)

United Nations Specialised Agencies

UNICEF   WHO

Choose **one** of the UN Specialised Agencies shown above.

Describe **two** ways in which the Agency you have chosen tries to meet the needs of many people in Africa.

(Knowledge and Understanding, **4** marks)

(b)

> In 2003, the United Kingdom gave farming equipment to several African countries as part of an aid package.

Give **two** reasons why the UK may benefit from giving aid to African countries.

(Knowledge and Understanding, **4** marks)

[Turn over

QUESTION 4 (CONTINUED)

(*c*)   Study the information below and then answer the question which follows.

Timeline—Zimbabwe	
Key Events 2000–2002	
Date	**Event**
February 2000	With the support of the Government, blacks seize hundreds of farms owned by whites. This is part of a campaign to take back land they believe was stolen from them by white farmers.
July 2001	Zimbabwe facing massive food shortages.
February 2002	All European Union countries cut trade links with Zimbabwe because of land policy.
April 2002	Very little food available legally but it can easily be bought on the "black market". However, "black market" prices are four times the normal rate.
May 2002	Worsening food shortages turning into a famine. The World Food Programme blames the land policy for this.
June 2002	2900 white farmers ordered to stop working and to leave within 45 days.

Adapted from BBC website

Statements made in a speech by Khalif–al–Toure

- The Government of Zimbabwe has helped white farmers.
- World Food Programme blames the land policy for the famine in Zimbabwe.
- It is only the UK government which has cut trade links because of the changing land policy.
- Food is available on the "black market" but it is very expensive.

Using **only** the information above, write down **two** statements by Khalif-al-Toure which are **exaggerated**.

Using the Timeline, give **one** reason why each of the statements you have chosen is **exaggerated**.

You must only use the information above.

(Enquiry Skills, **4** marks)

QUESTION 4 (CONTINUED)

(d)   Study the information below then answer the question which follows.

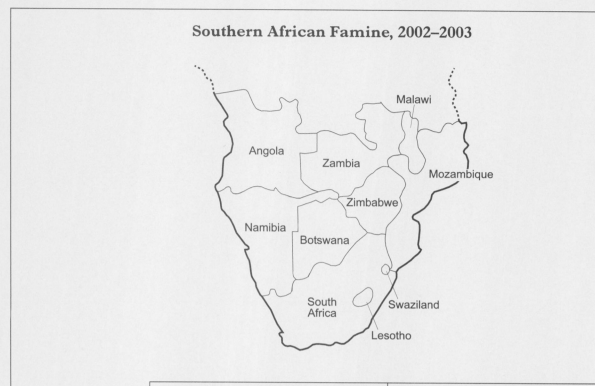

Southern African Famine, 2002–2003

	July 2002		March 2003	
	Affected by famine		*Affected by famine*	
	Number	*% of Population*	*Number*	*% of Population*
Angola	1·0 million	10	1·5 million	15
Malawi	0·5 million	5	3·2 million	30
Mozambique	0·4 million	2	0·5 million	3
Zambia	1·3 million	12	2·4 million	25
Zimbabwe	5·3 million	47	6·1 million	54

Write down **two conclusions** that can be reached about the famine in Southern Africa.

You should write **one** conclusion about **each** of the following.

- The country worst affected by famine in July 2002

- The changes that have taken place in the countries affected by famine between July 2002 and March 2003

Your conclusions must be based entirely on the information above.

(Enquiry Skills, **4** marks)

[END OF QUESTION PAPER]

[BLANK PAGE]

[BLANK PAGE]

C

2640/403

NATIONAL
QUALIFICATIONS
2004

MONDAY, 24 MAY
1.00 PM – 3.00 PM

MODERN STUDIES
STANDARD GRADE
Credit Level

1   Read every question carefully.

2   Answer all questions as fully as you can.

3   If you cannot do a question, go on to the next one. Try again later.

4   In question 3, answer **one** section only: Section (A) The USA **or** Section (B) Russia **or** Section (C) China.

5   Write your answers in the answer book provided. Indicate clearly, in the left hand margin, the question and section of question being answered. Do not write in the right hand margin.

SCOTTISH
QUALIFICATIONS
AUTHORITY

THB 2640/403 6/14920   ©

SYLLABUS AREA 1—LIVING IN A DEMOCRACY

QUESTION 1

(a) | *Pressure groups in the UK have **rights and responsibilities** in any actions they take in trying to influence public opinion and Government policy.*

Describe, **in detail**, the **rights and responsibilities** of pressure groups.

Answers **must** refer to specific Pressure Groups you have studied.

(Knowledge & Understanding, **8** marks)

(b) Study the cartoon below, then answer the question which follows.

Using **only** the cartoon above, what **conclusions** can be reached about the attitudes of people towards elections?

You must reach **two** separate conclusions.

Enquiry Skills, **4** marks)

QUESTION 1 (CONTINUED)

(*c*)   Study the information below, then answer the question which follows.

Average Number of Parliamentary Questions Asked By Each MSP in the Scottish Parliament (By Party) — 2001

Oral Questions

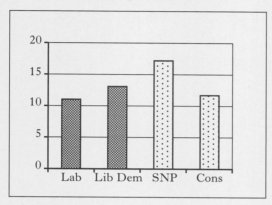

Written Questions

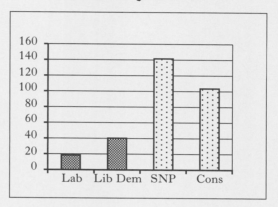

First Minister's Questions

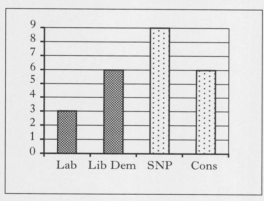

Composition of the Scottish Parliament	
Party	MSPs
Executive Coalition Parties ▨	
Labour/Lib Dem	72
Opposition Parties ⬚	
SNP	34
Conservative	19
Others	4

The main opposition party asks more Parliamentary Questions than the Executive Coalition parties put together.

View of Willie McKay

Give **one** reason to **support** and **one** reason to **oppose** the view of Willie McKay.

Overall, do you agree with Willie McKay? **Explain your answer**.

(Enquiry Skills, **6** marks)

[Turn over

SYLLABUS AREA 2—CHANGING SOCIETY

QUESTION 2

(a) | *Some older people in the UK live in housing that does not meet their* **needs**.

Explain, **in detail**, why *some older people in the UK live in housing that does not meet their* **needs**.

(Knowledge and Understanding, **4** marks)

(b) | *People with young children may have limited job opportunities.*

Explain, **in detail**, why *people with young children may have limited job opportunities.*

(Knowledge and Understanding, **4** marks)

QUESTION 2 (CONTINUED)

You have been asked to carry out an investigation into the topic in the box below.

> ## Changing technology and work.

Now answer questions (*c*), (*d*), (*e*) and (*f*).

(*c*) State a relevant **hypothesis** for your investigation.

(Enquiry Skills, **2** marks)

(*d*) Give **two** relevant **aims** or **headings** to help you prove or disprove your hypothesis.

(Enquiry Skills, **2** marks)

To help with your investigation you decide to **interview** the manager of a local factory.

(*e*) Describe the steps you would take to **arrange a visit** to the factory to conduct your interview.

(Enquiry Skills, **2** marks)

(*f*) Describe, **in detail**, the **advantages and disadvantages** of **interviewing** the manager as a method for your investigation.

(Enquiry Skills, **4** marks)

[Turn over

[BLANK PAGE]

SYLLABUS AREA 3—IDEOLOGIES

QUESTION 3

Answer **one** section only: Section (A) — The USA on pages *seven* to *ten*
          OR   Section (B) — Russia on pages *eleven* to *fourteen*
          OR   Section (C) — China on pages *fifteen* to *eighteen*

(A) **THE USA**

(*a*)

> *American citizens can participate in elections.*

Describe, **in detail**, the ways in which *American citizens can participate in elections.*

In your answer you **must** refer to American examples of participation in elections.

(Knowledge and Understanding, **8** marks)

[Turn over

QUESTION 3 (A) (CONTINUED)

(b)   Study the information below, then answer the question which follows on page *nine*.

HEALTH IN THE USA — A RECORD TO BE PROUD OF?

Good health and equality of health are important in a modern country. Between 1900 and 2000, life expectancy in the USA increased from 51 to 80 for females and from 48 to 74 for males. The Census Bureau estimates that life expectancy will be 87 for females and 81 for males by 2050.

One criticism of the health record of the USA is the link between poor health and factors such as education and gender. Men continue to have a worse death rate than women, and women have lower mortality rates at every age. Mortality rates improved more for women than for men. The gender gap in life expectancy actually increased. The number of years of education is also important. Men who have under 12 years of education have a death rate of 764 per 100 000 but if they have more than 13 years of education the death rate drops to 264. The pattern for women is similar — 410 and 173 per 100 000 depending on the number of years of education.

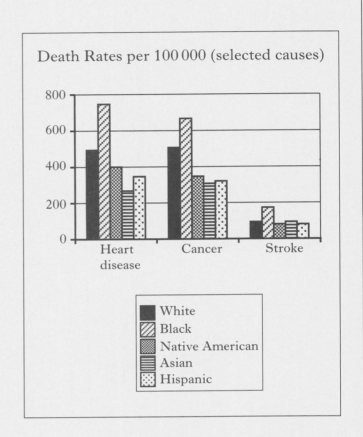

Death Rates per 100 000 (selected causes)

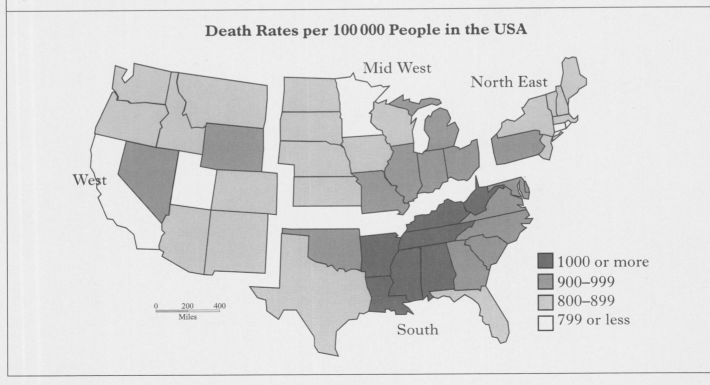

Death Rates per 100 000 People in the USA

QUESTION 3 (A) (*b*) (CONTINUED)

Location, education and race have little effect on health in the USA.

View of Hilary Wallace

Using **only** the information on page *eight*, explain **the extent to which** Hilary Wallace could be accused of being **selective in the use of facts**.

(Enquiry Skills, **6** marks)

[Turn over

QUESTION 3 (A) (CONTINUED)

(c)   Study the information below, then answer the question which follows.

Selected Information on Asian Immigration to the USA				
Region	**Where recent immigrants have settled (%)**	**Average Hourly Earnings ($)**	**Percentage of the population who are Asian**	**US–Asian owned firms (%)***
New England	3	17·5	2·7	2·4
Middle Atlantic	22	18·7	4·4	19·8
East North Central	8	16·1	2·0	7·5
West North Central	2	15·0	1·6	1·8
South Atlantic	15	15·2	2·1	12·4
East South Central	1	15·0	0·8	1·5
West South Central	11	15·1	2·2	7·9
Mountain	4	14·7	1·9	3·1
Pacific	34	17·7	10·3	43·6

*This column refers to the percentage of all businesses owned by US–Asians that are located in each region.

Using **only** the information above, give **two** conclusions about the reasons why recent Asian immigrants are more likely to settle in certain regions of the USA.

(Enquiry Skills, **4** marks)

NOW GO TO QUESTION 4 ON PAGE NINETEEN

QUESTION 3 (CONTINUED)

(B) **RUSSIA**

(a) | *Russian citizens can participate in elections.* |

Describe, **in detail**, the ways in which *Russian citizens can participate in elections*.

In your answer you **must** refer to Russian examples of participation in elections.

(Knowledge and Understanding, **8** marks)

[Turn over

QUESTION 3 (B) (CONTINUED)

(b)   Study the information below, then answer the question which follows on page *thirteen*.

CRISIS FOR HEALTH STANDARDS IN RUSSIA

The Soviet Union broke up into several independent states in the early 1990s. These include Russia, Belarus, Ukraine and Estonia. The system of health care in Russia is in danger of collapsing. Back in the Communist period, hospitals and health care were generously funded with large state subsidies. Now, in the free-market economy, health care has been starved of resources. A system that was the envy of the rest of the world has become a source of shame.

The standard of health care a person can expect varies depending on where they live. People from major cities such as Moscow and St Petersburg enjoy a level of care that is better than anywhere in the whole of the former Soviet Union. However, in remote areas of the north and east of Russia, health care standards are very poor. In the far east of Russia some people live more than 200 miles from the nearest hospital.

Medical services in countries such as Estonia, Ukraine and Belarus have benefited from closer links with Europe. Russia has been slower to make these links and standards have suffered.

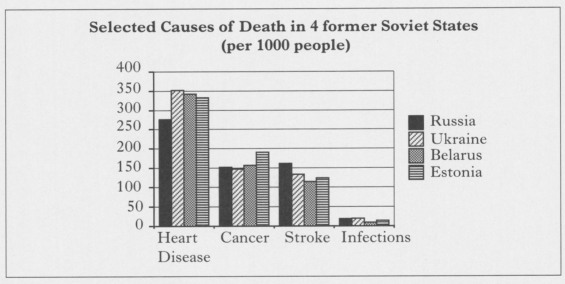

Selected Causes of Death in 4 former Soviet States (per 1000 people)

Legend: Russia, Ukraine, Belarus, Estonia

Categories: Heart Disease, Cancer, Stroke, Infections

Health-related Statistics in 4 former Soviet States	Crude Death Rate (per 1000 people)	Life Expectancy at Birth	Mothers who die in childbirth (per 100 000 births)	Infant Mortality rate (per 1000 births)
Russia	16	65	75	15
Ukraine	15	68	45	12
Belarus	14	69	33	9
Estonia	14	71	80	9

QUESTION 3 (B) (*b*) (CONTINUED)

Health standards in Russia are worse than in other former Soviet states.

View of Olga Davidova

Using **only** the information on page *twelve*, explain **the extent to which** Olga Davidova could be accused of being **selective in the use of facts**.

(Enquiry Skills, **6** marks)

[Turn over

QUESTION 3 (B) (CONTINUED)

(*c*)   Study the information below then answer the question which follows.

Selected Information on Education in autonomous Republics within Russia

Republic	Population (million)	Number of General Schools	Number of Vocational Schools	Number of Higher Schools
Bashkortostan	4·0	3264	157	9
Buryatia	1·1	602	44	4
Chuvashia	1·4	715	35	3
Dagestan	2·1	1589	29	5
Karelia	0·8	336	21	3
Komi	1·2	591	12	1
Sakha	1·1	711	33	2
Tatarstan	3·8	2422	118	15
Udmurtia	1·5	882	45	15

Using **only** the information above, give **two** conclusions about the provision of different types of school in the autonomous republics.

(Enquiry Skills, **4** marks)

NOW GO TO QUESTION 4 ON PAGE NINETEEN

QUESTION 3 (CONTINUED)

(C) **CHINA**

(a) | *Chinese citizens would like more freedom to participate in elections.* |

Describe, **in detail**, the ways in which *Chinese citizens could participate more fully in elections if they were given more freedom.*

In your answer you **must** refer to Chinese examples.

(Knowledge and Understanding, **8** marks)

[Turn over

QUESTION 3 (C) (CONTINUED)

(b) Study the information below, then answer the question which follows on page *seventeen*.

EDUCATION IN CHINA — A RECORD TO BE PROUD OF?

In 1990, the average class size for secondary schools was 15 and for primary schools it was 22. In 2000, the average class size for secondary schools in China was 17. In primary schools the figure was 24.

However, the actual number of teachers in both primary and secondary sectors increased between 1990 and 2000. In 1990, there were 3·5 million secondary teachers and 5·6 million primary teachers. By 2000, this had increased to 4·3 million secondary teachers and 5·8 million in primary schools.

The changing pupil-teacher ratio must be explained by increasing numbers of children attending school. This is mainly because more youngsters are enrolling in schools and staying on longer. The effect of the One Child Policy has also been less than the government expected.

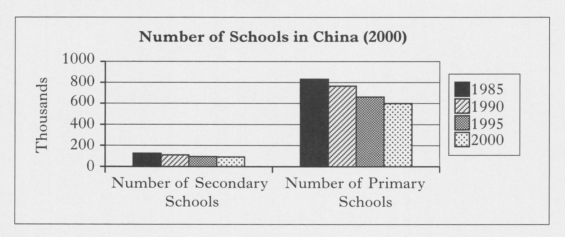

Number of Schools in China (2000)

Legend: 1985, 1990, 1995, 2000

Selected Education Statistics for Provinces of Southern China (2000)

Province	Proportion of China's Population (%)	Proportion of University Graduates (%)
a Guizhou	2·9	1·2
b Guangxi	3·7	2·2
c Hunan	5·2	4·5
d Guangdong	5·6	5·9
e Fujian	2·7	2·6
f Jiangxi	3·3	2·8

QUESTION 3 (C) (*b*) (CONTINUED)

Education statistics in China show a steady improvement. Educational achievement in Southern China is particularly good.

View of Jiang Zhi

Using **only** the information on page *sixteen*, explain **the extent to which** Jiang Zhi could be accused of being **selective in the use of facts.**

(Enquiry Skills, **6** marks)

[Turn over

QUESTION 3 (C) (CONTINUED)

(c)   Study the information below then answer the question which follows.

Information about Crime in Hong Kong

Reported Crimes by Type of Offence			
	1996	**2000**	**2001**
Violent Crime	15 191	14 812	13 551
Non-violent crime	63 859	62 433	59 457
Total	79 050	77 245	73 008
Overall crime rate (per 100 000 population)	1228	1159	1086
Violent crime rate (per 100 000 population)	236	222	202
Persons arrested by Type of Offence			
	1996	**2000**	**2001**
Violent Crime	9910	9497	8435
Non-violent crime	37 247	31 433	30 394
Total	47 157	40 930	38 829
Rate of persons arrested for crime (per 100 000 population)	798	659	617

Using **only** the information above, what **conclusions** can be reached about crime in Hong Kong?

You **must** reach **one** conclusion about each of the following:

* detection rates for different types of crime (proportions of crime for which arrests are made)

* changes in crime statistics since 1996.

(Enquiry Skills, **4** marks)

NOW GO TO QUESTION 4 ON PAGE NINETEEN

SYLLABUS AREA 4—INTERNATIONAL RELATIONS

QUESTION 4

(*a*)

> *European countries have taken security measures to protect themselves against threats such as international terrorism.*

Describe, **in detail**, some of the *security measures taken by European countries to protect themselves against threats such as international terrorism.*

(Knowledge and Understanding, **4** marks)

(*b*)

> *Countries joining the European Union (EU) recently have done so for economic reasons.*

Explain, **in detail**, the *economic reasons for countries joining the European Union (EU).*

(Knowledge and Understanding, **4** marks)

[Turn over

QUESTION 4 (CONTINUED)

(*c*) Study sources 1, 2 and 3 below and opposite, then answer the question which follows.

Aims of the International Criminal Tribunal for the former Yugoslavia (ICTY)

The ICTY was established by the UN Security Council in 1993. Its main aims are:

1. to bring to justice the people mainly responsible for crimes against humanity, including genocide;
2. to try to stop further war crimes by showing the world that individuals will be prosecuted;
3. to help restore peace by promoting good relations between former enemies;
4. to be even-handed and deal equally with war crimes committed by all sides.

SOURCE 1

Selected factual Information on the ICTY (2002)

*   Slobodan Milosevic, former President of the Federal Republic of Yugoslavia, was the most high profile detainee. He was charged with crimes against humanity including deportation, murder and persecution of thousands of people from Kosovo.
*   Most of the other detainees were low ranking military personnel charged with carrying out killings under the orders of more senior officials.
*   Most sentences handed out by the court have been between 2 years to 10 years imprisonment. However, one person got 25 years and another got 40 years.

What happened to the people who have been detained by the ICTY?

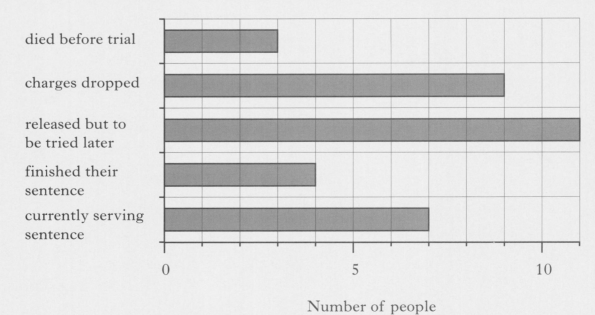

QUESTION 4 (*c*) (CONTINUED)

SOURCE 2

NATO WAR CRIMES IN YUGOSLAVIA

Milosevic and other Serbs are on trial for crimes against humanity, genocide and war crimes. However, Serbian people remember the crimes committed by NATO during its illegal campaign against Yugoslavia in 1999. NATO bombs, sanctioned by the UN, killed more than 500 Serbian civilians.

The ICTY must be independent in its pursuit of war criminals. The vast majority of people detained so far are Serbians. No-one working for the UN or NATO has been charged. It must investigate the political and military leadership of NATO including Bill Clinton and Tony Blair. Only then will the people of Serbia feel that real justice has been handed out and peace can return to the country.

Adapted from *Pravda on-line*

SOURCE 3

FRESH EVIDENCE OF WAR CRIMES IN YUGOSLAVIA

When the Serbians were forced to withdraw from Muslim areas of Bosnia, the evidence of war crimes was there for all to see. They had embarked on a policy of "ethnic cleansing" aimed at forcing the Muslim population out of certain towns and areas. The worst massacre was the one at Srebrenica in 1995 where approximately eight thousand Muslim males simply "disappeared". By 2002, the commander of the Serb forces responsible had not been arrested. In total, thousands of Serbians took part in war crimes.

More recently, the arrival of UN and NATO forces in Kosovo has uncovered more evidence of war crimes. Once again, the Serbians had tried a policy of ethnic cleansing — this time aimed against Albanians in the Kosovo region. The Serbian government had released criminals from jails in Belgrade on condition that they join para-military death squads. Thousands of Albanians were killed in Kosovo.

Many Serbians, the group who started the conflict, still support extreme political groups. There are no plans to withdraw UN and NATO peacekeepers from the former Yugoslavia at present — the situation remains very tense. The small number of prosecutions by the ICTY leaves the people of Kosovo worried about the future.

Adapted from *Kosovo watch* web site

The International Criminal Tribunal for the Former Yugoslavia (ICTY) has met each of its aims.

View of Tomas Moller

Using **only** information about the aims of the ICTY and Sources 1–3 above and opposite, give **detailed** reasons **for** and **against** the view of Tomas Moller.

(Enquiry Skills, **8** marks)

(*d*)   Overall, do you **agree** with Tomas Moller? **Explain** why you have reached this decision.

(Enquiry Skills, **2** marks)

[END OF QUESTION PAPER]

[BLANK PAGE]

[BLANK PAGE]

G

2640/402

NATIONAL
QUALIFICATIONS
2005

MONDAY, 23 MAY
10.20 AM–11.50 AM

MODERN STUDIES
STANDARD GRADE
General Level

1   Read every question carefully.

2   Answer all questions as fully as you can.

3   If you cannot do a question, go on to the next one. Try again later.

4   In question 3, answer **one** section only; Section (A) The USA **or** Section (B) Russia **or** Section (C) China.

5   Write your answers in the answer book provided. Indicate clearly, in the left hand margin, the question and section of question being answered. Do not write in the right hand margin.

SCOTTISH
QUALIFICATIONS
AUTHORITY

©

SYLLABUS AREA 1—LIVING IN A DEMOCRACY

QUESTION 1

(a) | *Pressure groups can take different actions to try to influence the Government.* |

Describe **two** actions which *pressure groups can take to try to influence the Government.*

(Knowledge & Understanding, **4** marks)

(b) Study the information below, then answer the question which follows.

Survey of People who did not Vote in the Scottish Parliament Election (2003)

Question 1: Why did you not vote?

	Percentage Agreeing
I meant to vote but circumstances prevented me	45
The parties are all the same	37
The Scottish Parliament cannot do very much	35
I am not interested	36
Obvious who would win so no point in voting	21

Question 2: Which new voting method would make you more likely to vote?

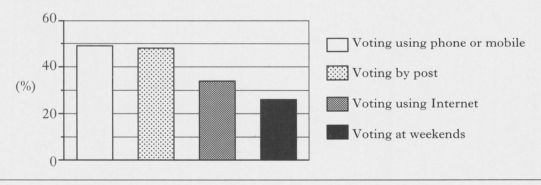

- Voting using phone or mobile
- Voting by post
- Voting using Internet
- Voting at weekends

Statements by Meena Patel about people who do not vote

- Almost everyone says that the parties are all the same.
- Nearly half of the people would have voted but circumstances prevented them.
- Using the Internet would be the most likely way to increase voting.
- More people would vote if they could use their phone or mobile.

Using **only** the information above, write down **two** statements made by Meena Patel which are **exaggerated**.

Using the information, give **one** reason why **each** of the statements you have chosen is **exaggerated**.

(Enquiry Skills, **4** marks)

QUESTION 1 (CONTINUED)

You are investigating the topic in the box below.

> ### The work of a Local Councillor

Answer questions (*c*), (*d*) and (*e*) which follow.

(*c*)   As part of the **Planning Stage**, give **two** relevant **aims** for your investigation.

(Enquiry Skills, **2** marks)

You see the following advertisement in the local paper.

Study the advertisement carefully, then answer the question which follows.

Mary Millar, Inverdee Councillor
Answering Your Questions / Solving Your Problems

Surgeries will be held as follows:

Inverdee Town Hall

7.00 – 9.00 pm, first and third Tuesday each month
(No appointment required)

Inverdee Secondary School

7.00 – 9.00 pm, second and fourth Tuesday each month
(No appointment required)

Contact Mary Millar
Inverdee City Council Offices
Inverbrig Road
Inverdee
Phone: Inverdee 207086
e-mail: mmillar@inverdeecouncil.gov.uk

My door is always open

(*d*)   You have decided to try and contact a local councillor to help you in your investigation.

From the advertisement above, choose **two** ways in which you could contact a local councillor.

For **each** way you have chosen, explain why it is a **good** way to get information to help in your investigation.

(Enquiry Skills, **4** marks)

(*e*)   You also decide to use copies of your local newspaper from the past two years to help with your investigation.

Give **one** advantage and **one** disadvantage of using **past copies of the local newspaper** for your investigation.

(Enquiry Skills, **2** marks)

SYLLABUS AREA 2—CHANGING SOCIETY

QUESTION 2

(a)

> *The Government has tried to reduce poverty amongst families.*

Describe **two** recent Government policies which try *to reduce poverty amongst families.*

(Knowledge & Understanding, **4** marks)

(b)

> *Some elderly people can afford housing that is ideal for their needs.*

Give **two** reasons why *some elderly people can afford housing that is ideal for their needs.*

(Knowledge & Understanding, **4** marks)

(c)   Study the information below, then answer the question which follows.

Survey of Employed People **The way in which you found out about your current job (%)**		
	Male	*Female*
Hearing from someone who works there	31	25
Replying to advertisement in newspaper	24	33
Making direct contact with employer	14	16
Through a private employment agency	11	9
By visiting the Job Centre	9	7
Some other way	11	10

Few people find out about their job through the Job Centre. Responding to advertisements in newspapers is the most common way of finding out about a job for both men and women.

View of David Reid

Using **only** the information above, give **one** reason to **support** and **one** reason to **oppose** the view of David Reid.

(Enquiry Skills, **4** marks)

QUESTION 2 (CONTINUED)

(*d*)   Study the information below, then answer the question which follows.

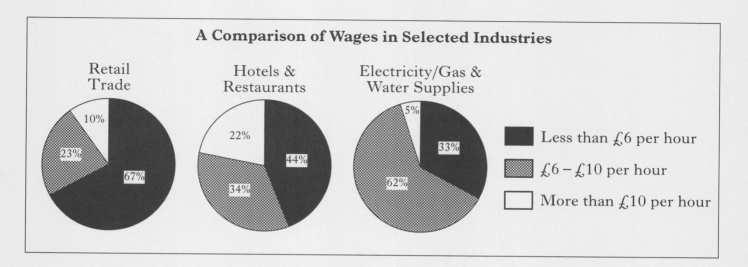

A Comparison of Wages in Selected Industries

Retail Trade — 10%, 23%, 67%

Hotels & Restaurants — 22%, 34%, 44%

Electricity/Gas & Water Supplies — 5%, 33%, 62%

■ Less than £6 per hour

▨ £6 – £10 per hour

□ More than £10 per hour

Write down **two** conclusions that can be reached about differences in wages between the selected industries.

You **must** only use the information above.

(Enquiry Skills, **4** marks)

[Turn over

SYLLABUS AREA 3—IDEOLOGIES

QUESTION 3

Answer **ONE** section only: Section (A)—The USA on pages *six* and *seven*

OR Section (B)—Russia on pages *eight* and *nine*

OR Section (C)—China on pages *ten* and *eleven*

(A) **THE USA**

(a)

> *American people have political rights and responsibilities.*

Describe **one** political right which American people have **and** the responsibility that goes with it.

In your answer you **must** refer to American examples.

(Knowledge & Understanding, **4** marks)

(b)

> *Many American people have started up their own businesses.*

Give **two** reasons why *many American people have started up their own businesses.*

In your answer you **must** refer to American examples.

(Knowledge & Understanding, **4** marks)

(c) Study the information below, then answer the question which follows.

USA—Student Dentists by Ethnic Group		
Ethnic Group	*1992*	*2002*
White	11,185	11,176
African American	940	808
Hispanic	1,254	912
Asian	2,519	4,317
Native American	53	99

Statements from a speech by George Plant

- The number of White students has gone down by a large amount.

- Numbers of both Asian and Native American students have increased significantly.

- In 2002, there were more White students than all other groups put together.

- The biggest decline in student dentists has been for African Americans.

Using **only** the information above, write down **two** statements made by George Plant which are **exaggerated**.

Using the information, give **one** reason why **each** of the statements you have chosen is **exaggerated**.

(Enquiry Skills, **4** marks)

QUESTION 3 (A) (CONTINUED)

(d)   Study Sources 1 and 2 below, then answer the question which follows.

SOURCE 1

**Extract from an Election Speech by Democratic Party Candidate,
November 2004**

In this election, Americans must make important decisions about the direction our country should take. For example, some people cannot afford health care insurance. We must expand Government schemes such as Medicare to help them.

This may mean an increase in tax. However, I think most people will accept this increase if it is used to improve public services such as health and education. It is important that everyone votes to make sure that their views are put forward.

SOURCE 2

**Extract from an Election Speech by a Republican Party Candidate,
November 2004**

Our nation is the richest in the world because of our free market economy. People who work hard want to be allowed to keep their money and not have it taken away from them by the Government in higher taxes.

The Government has got many things to spend its money on. The best way of achieving good health care for all is by encouraging private medical insurance. If you vote for me, I'll make sure the job is done.

Sources 1 and 2 give information about **the different policies of candidates at the 2004 American elections**.

Write down **two** of the **differences** between the policies of these candidates.

You **must** only use information from the Sources above.

(Enquiry Skills, **4** marks)

NOW GO TO QUESTION 4 ON PAGE TWELVE

QUESTION 3 (CONTINUED)

(B) **RUSSIA**

(*a*)

> *Russian people have political rights and responsibilities.*

Describe **one** political right which Russian people have **and** the responsibility that goes with it.

In your answer you **must** refer to Russian examples.

(Knowledge & Understanding, **4** marks)

(*b*)

> *The Russian Government has encouraged people to start up their own businesses.*

Give **two** reasons why *the Russian Government has encouraged people to start up their own businesses.*

In your answer you **must** refer to Russian examples.

(Knowledge & Understanding, **4** marks)

(*c*) Study the information below, then answer the question which follows.

Russia—Selected Health Statistics		
	2000	*2001*
Number of doctors (thousands)	683	682
Number of nurses (thousands)	1,612	1,564
Number of hospitals (thousands)	11	10
Number of health centres (thousands)	21	21

Statements from a speech by Alexander Dassaev

- The number of doctors in Russia has gone down by a large amount.

- The number of both doctors and nurses has gone down.

- The total number of hospitals and health centres in Russia was less in 2000 than in 2001.

- As the number of doctors and nurses has fallen, so has the number of hospitals.

Using **only** the information above, write down **two** statements made by Alexander Dassaev which are **exaggerated**.

Using the information, give **one** reason why **each** of the statements you have chosen is **exaggerated**.

(Enquiry Skills, **4** marks)

QUESTION 3 (B) (CONTINUED)

(d)   Study Sources 1 and 2 below, then answer the question which follows.

SOURCE 1

Extract from an Election Speech by a Yabloko Candidate, December 2003

The Government needs to spend more time on improving health and education services. These are the most important issues for the voters.

We believe that the richest people in Russia should pay very high taxes on their incomes. However, people who made money back in the 1990s should not now have it taken away from them. They took big risks to help the Russian economy change from the Communist system to a Capitalist system.

SOURCE 2

Extract from an Election Speech by a Communist Party Candidate, December 2003

Taxes should be changed so that the very wealthy pay more. The gap between rich and poor in Russia is too great. People who made huge sums of money in the late 1990s should be made to pay back most of it to the Government.

The biggest issue at this election is Russia's foreign policy. Our country should not be making such strong links with the European Union and the USA.

Sources 1 and 2 give information about **the different policies of candidates at the 2003 Russian elections**.

Write down **two** of the **differences** between the policies of these candidates.

You **must** only use information from the Sources above.

(Enquiry Skills, **4** marks)

NOW GO TO QUESTION 4 ON PAGE TWELVE

QUESTION 3 (CONTINUED)

(C) **CHINA**

(a)
> *Chinese people have limited political rights.*

Describe **one** political right which Chinese people have.

Describe **one further** political right which many Chinese people would like to be given.

In your answer you **must** refer to Chinese examples.

(Knowledge & Understanding, **4** marks)

(b)
> *The Chinese Government has encouraged people to start up their own businesses.*

Give **two** reasons why *the Chinese Government has encouraged people to start up their own businesses.*

In your answer you **must** refer to Chinese examples.

(Knowledge & Understanding, **4** marks)

(c) Study the information below, then answer the question which follows.

China—Selected Health Statistics	*1999*	*2000*
Number of hospitals and clinics (thousands)	309	320
Number of doctors (thousands)	1,303	1,300
Number of nurses (thousands)	1,007	1,005
Official number of drug addicts (thousands)	572	681

Statements from a speech by Lee Quangxing

- The number of doctors in China has gone down by a large amount.
- The total number of nurses and doctors in China has gone down.
- The number of drug addicts went up by more than 100,000 between 1999 and 2000.
- The number of drug addicts in China has gone up while the numbers of hospitals and clinics has gone down.

Using **only** the information above, write down **two** statements made by Lee Quangxing which are **exaggerated**.

Using the information, give **one** reason why **each** of the statements you have chosen is **exaggerated**.

(Enquiry Skills, **4** marks)

QUESTION 3 (C) (CONTINUED)

(d) Study Sources 1 and 2 below, then answer the question which follows.

SOURCE 1

Extract from a Communist Party speech about Hong Kong

Elections were held in Hong Kong recently. All people had the opportunity to vote in a fair election. We need to have strong links with the Communist Party in China and to make similar laws. This will make our country stronger.

The Communist Party knows that Hong Kong must keep its special economic status. The Government needs to work with large businesses in Hong Kong to create more jobs. This is the biggest problem for the Government.

SOURCE 2

Extract from a Non-Communist Party (Dissident) speech about Hong Kong

The most important issue facing the Government in Hong Kong is how to create new jobs. Many jobs have been lost in recent years. Hong Kong must have the freedom to make economic decisions which are different from those in China. Hong Kong must keep its special economic status. This will be of great benefit.

The recent elections in Hong Kong were not free and fair. Hong Kong should be able to decide on its own laws and not have to follow the Communist Party in China.

Sources 1 and 2 give information about **the different policies of parties towards Hong Kong**.

Write down **two** of the **differences** between the policies of these parties.

You **must** only use information from the Sources above.

(Enquiry Skills, **4** marks)

NOW GO TO QUESTION 4 ON PAGE TWELVE

SYLLABUS AREA 4—INTERNATIONAL RELATIONS

QUESTION 4

(a) | *European countries such as the UK have been involved in international conflicts in recent years.*

Describe **two** ways in which *European countries such as the UK have been involved in international conflicts in recent years.*

In your answer, refer to examples that you have studied.

(Knowledge & Understanding, **4** marks)

(b) | *Many countries have joined the European Union recently.*

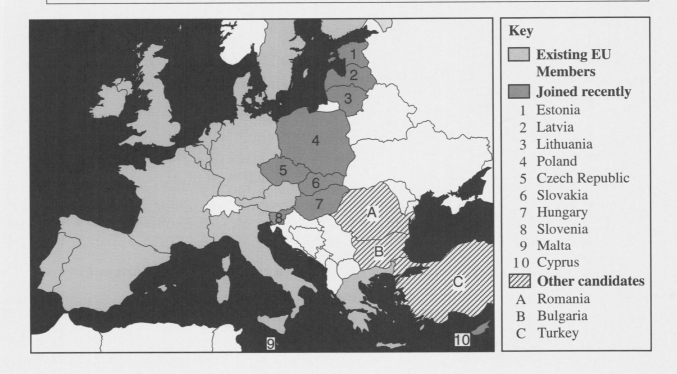

Give **two** reasons to explain why *many countries have joined the European Union recently*.

(Knowledge & Understanding, **4** marks)

QUESTION 4 (CONTINUED)

(c) Study Sources 1 and 2 below, then answer the question which follows.

SOURCE 1

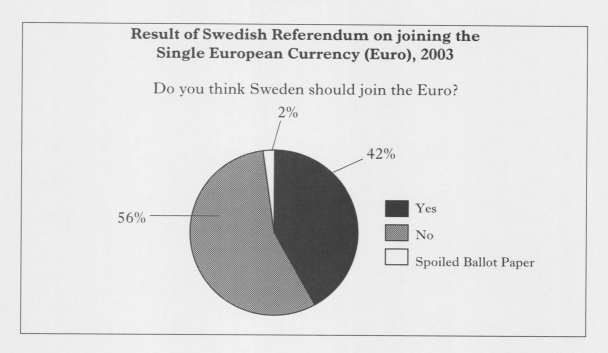

Result of Swedish Referendum on joining the Single European Currency (Euro), 2003

Do you think Sweden should join the Euro?

2%

42%

56%

Yes

No

Spoiled Ballot Paper

SOURCE 2

Newsfile, September 2003

Sweden has voted on the Single European Currency (Euro). There are currently 15 members of the EU and 12 of them belong to the Eurozone. Many Swedish businesses feel that they will lose trade because Sweden will not become part of the Eurozone and they may seek compensation from the Government. There will not be another referendum for 10 years.

The Swedish referendum did not produce a clear result. Swedish businesses were delighted with this result.

View of Katie Halfpenny, Economist

Using only Sources 1 and 2, give **two** reasons to **disagree** with the view of Katie Halfpenny.

(Enquiry Skills, **4** marks)

[Turn over for question 4(d) on Page fourteen

QUESTION 4 (CONTINUED)

(*d*) Study the information below, then answer the question which follows.

Aid donated by Selected Countries, 2000 and 2001 (in US million dollars)		
Donor Country	*2000*	*2001*
Austria	423	533
Denmark	1,664	1,634
Germany	5,030	4,990
Japan	13,508	9,847
New Zealand	113	112
UK	4,501	4,579
USA	9,955	11,429

Write down **two** conclusions about the **changes** in aid donated by selected countries.

You should write **one** conclusion about **each** of the following.

- The country giving most aid in 2001 compared to 2000
- The changes in the amount of aid given by different countries

You **must** only use the information above.

(Enquiry Skills, **4** marks)

[END OF QUESTION PAPER]

C

2640/403

NATIONAL
QUALIFICATIONS
2005

MONDAY, 23 MAY
1.00 PM – 3.00 PM

MODERN STUDIES
STANDARD GRADE
Credit Level

1   Read every question carefully.

2   Answer all questions as fully as you can.

3   If you cannot do a question, go on to the next one. Try again later.

4   In question 3, answer **one** section only: Section (A) The USA **or** Section (B) Russia **or** Section (C) China.

5   Write your answers in the answer book provided. Indicate clearly, in the left hand margin, the question and section of question being answered. Do not write in the right hand margin.

SCOTTISH
QUALIFICATIONS
AUTHORITY

©

[BLANK PAGE]

SYLLABUS AREA 1—LIVING IN A DEMOCRACY

QUESTION 1

(a)
> *Our elected representatives work on behalf of people in many different ways.*

Choose **either** Local Councillors **or** MSPs **or** MPs.

Describe, **in detail**, the ways in which the type of representative you have chosen works on behalf of the people they represent.

(Knowledge & Understanding, **6** marks)

(b)   Study the information below, then answer the question which follows.

Proportion of workers who are trade union members (Great Britain 1990–2000)

	1990	1995	2000
Number of union members (thousands)	8835	7309	7321
All employment	33·9%	28·8%	27%
Gender			
Male	44%	35%	30%
Female	32%	30%	29%
Type of work			
Manual	42%	33%	28%
Non-manual	35%	32%	30%
Full- or part-time work			
Full-time	43%	36%	33%
Part-time	22%	21%	23%
Employment Sector			
Manufacturing	44%	34%	28%
Services	37%	33%	31%

> Trade unions have become more gender equal since 1990. Unions are now strongest in manual work and the manufacturing sector despite recent changes in British industry.

View of Frances Naismith

Using **only** the information above, give **one** reason to **support** and **one** reason to **oppose** the view of Frances Naismith.

(Enquiry Skills, **4** marks)

QUESTION 1 (CONTINUED)

(c) Study Sources 1, 2 and 3 below and opposite, then answer the question which follows.

SOURCE 1

The UK Population	
Age profile (% of the age group 20–59)	2001
20–29	23·7
30–39	29·5
40–49	24·4
50–59	22·4
Total	**100%**

Educational Background	2001
School only	79·4
FE College	7·2
University	13·4
Total	**100%**

Occupational Background	2001
Manual workers	52·3
Financial and business	19·0
Public administration, defence, legal, political	5·4
Education, social work, health	18·3
Other	5·0
Total	**100%**

Gender and Ethnic minority background

The UK population is 49% male and 51% female. The UK population is 94·5% white and 5·5% from ethnic minority backgrounds. In Scotland 96·5% are from white and 3·5% from ethnic minority backgrounds.

SOURCE 2

Westminster Parliament	
Age profile (MPs) (% of the age group 20–59)	2001
20–29	0·7
30–39	14·1
40–49	41·6
50–59	43·6
Total	**100%**

Educational Background (MPs)	2001
School only	8·7
FE College	16·5
University	74·8
Total	**100%**

Occupational Background (MPs)	2001
Manual workers	20·4
Financial and business	23·4
Public administration, defence, legal, political	36·6
Education, social work, health	17·6
Other	2·0
Total	**100%**

Gender and Ethnic minority background

In Westminster 17·9% of the MPs are female and 2% from an ethnic minority background which many people feel is not good enough.

QUESTION 1(c) (CONTINUED)

SOURCE 3

Scottish Parliament

Age profile of MSPs (% of the age group 20–59)	1999	2003
20–29	4·2	1·0
30–39	27·7	18·6
40–49	40·3	41·6
50–59	27·8	38·8
Total	**100%**	**100%**

Educational Background of MSPs	1999	2003
School only	8·1	8·6
FE College	18·5	15·5
University	73·4	75·9
Total	**100%**	**100%**

Occupational Background of MSPs	1999	2003
Manual workers	10·9	7·7
Financial and business	20·3	22·9
Public administration, defence, legal, political	27·4	22·5
Education, social work, health	28·1	33·6
Other	13·3	13·3
Total	**100%**	**100%**

Gender and Ethnic minority background

In the areas of gender and ethnic minority equality, the Scottish Parliament hoped that it would improve representation. The Scottish Parliament in 1999 was 63% male whilst in 2003 it was 60·5% male. Scottish Parliament MSPs were 100% white in both 1999 and 2003.

It was hoped that one of the successes of the Scottish Parliament, when comparing it to the Westminster Parliament, would be in achieving fairer representation for all groups.

Using **only** the information in Sources 1, 2 and 3 above and opposite, what conclusions can be reached about **the success of the Scottish Parliament, when comparing it to the Westminster Parliament, in achieving fairer representation for all groups?**

You must reach conclusions about **four** of the following headings. For **each** conclusion, you must refer in each case to Sources 1, 2 and 3.

- Women
- People from an ethnic minority background
- People under 40
- People without further and higher education qualifications
- Manual workers

(Enquiry Skills, **8** marks)

[BLANK PAGE]

SYLLABUS AREA 2—CHANGING SOCIETY

QUESTION 2

(a) | *Getting a job is a challenge for young people. Many young people need help which is available from Central Government, local Councils and voluntary organisations.*

Describe **two** different ways in which **either** Central Government **or** local Councils **or** voluntary organisations help young people to get a job.

For **each** way, explain why it might be effective in helping a young person get a job.

(Knowledge and Understanding, **6** marks)

(b) | *Some people prefer to work from home for a variety of reasons. Technology allows them to do this.*

Explain, **in detail**, the reasons why *some people prefer to work from home.*

In answering this question you **must** refer to:

• the needs of some people

• the technology available.

(Knowledge and Understanding, **4** marks)

[Turn over

QUESTION 2 (CONTINUED)

(*c*) Study Sources 1, 2 and 3 below and opposite, then answer the question which follows.

SOURCE 1

Population of Scotland in 2000 (Selected Age Ranges)

	Number (000s)	% of total pop
45 – 64	1212	23·7
65 – 74	440	8·6
75+	347	6·8
Total population	5115	100

SOURCE 2

TABLE 1

Annual numbers of consultations with primary care health workers in Scotland in 2000 (figures in thousands)

	Age 45–54	Age 55–64	Age 65+
Doctor	2272	1967	3769
Practice Nurse	783	784	1600
Health Visitor	30	40	288
District Nurse	231	275	1989

TABLE 2

Day patient and inpatient admission rates; by age group: Scotland 2000

	Annual rates per 1000 population		
	Day Patients	Inpatients (more than 1 day)	
		Planned Admissions	Emergency Admissions
Males			
45–54	83	40	80
55–64	133	77	124
65–74	184	118	194
75–84	206	143	322
85+	170	137	498
Females			
45–54	101	51	62
55–64	129	69	86
65–74	146	87	145
75–84	136	94	155
85+	98	90	427

QUESTION 2(c) (CONTINUED)

SOURCE 3

Simply the best or not?

Comments from some over 65s on their experiences of the National Health Service (NHS) in Scotland.

• My wife has had a lot of treatment on the NHS. The NHS has been wonderful for us.

Harold, 75

• There was no effort to ensure that I had adequate back-up at home after I left the hospital.

Elsie, 73

• It's hard to get a doctor as you've far too long to wait for an appointment.

George, 73

• The emergency treatment was excellent. Rushed to hospital within ten minutes and seen by a doctor within another two or three minutes.

Mildred, 68

What over 65s think of health care services in Scotland (2003)

	In need of a lot of Improvement %	In need of some Improvement %	Satisfactory %	Very Good %
Quality of medical treatment in hospitals	12	39	41	8
Quality of nursing care in hospitals	12	30	37	21
General condition of hospital buildings	18	39	36	7
Quality of medical treatment by your local doctor	7	23	51	19

The elderly are the biggest users of the NHS in Scotland and they are satisfied with the quality of health care they receive.

View of Norman Macphail

Using **only** Sources 1, 2 and 3, explain **the extent to which** Norman Macphail could be accused of being **selective in the use of facts**.

(Enquiry Skills, **8** marks)

[BLANK PAGE]

SYLLABUS AREA 3—IDEOLOGIES

QUESTION 3

Answer **one** section only: Section (A)—The USA on pages *eleven* to *thirteen*
                              OR   Section (B)—Russia on pages *fifteen* to *seventeen*
                              OR   Section (C)—China on pages *nineteen* to *twenty-one*

(A) **THE USA**

(*a*) | *There continues to be social and economic inequality in the USA.* |

Explain, **in detail**, why there is *social and economic inequality* in the USA.

In your answer you **must** use American examples.

(Knowledge and Understanding, **8** marks)

[Turn over

QUESTION 3 (A) (CONTINUED)

(b) Study the information about Rockford City below. Also study the information in Sources 1 and 2 opposite. Sources 1 and 2 contain information about the two people who are candidates to become Mayor of Rockford City.

Information about Rockford City

- Rockford City is a small city of about 21 000 people. It is situated in the Eastern USA, about an hour's drive away from Raleigh, the state capital. It is a wealthy community with incomes well above the national average. However, there are a number of issues which concern local people.

- The proposed new Red Pine commercial project will provide a range of shopping, recreation and dining opportunities. Most local people believe that this will help economic growth, attracting shoppers from other towns. However, at present the site is an attractive wood used by local people for leisure.

- There are over 7000 students attending the 5 Elementary, 3 Middle and 2 High schools in Rockford City. The standard of education is good but Rockford High school is old and in poor condition. It is due to be rebuilt and most residents want to see it being turned into a magnet school which will promote racial diversity and offer better course options.

- Public transport is poor and most people make extensive use of their cars. However, the condition of many roads has been criticised—especially in housing areas where there are many potholes causing damage to cars. There have also been calls to improve the main road to the state capital to help commuters and attract new jobs to the city.

- In 2003, Hurricane Isobel caused serious flooding in the area. As a result many homes and businesses were damaged and it is estimated that it will cost over $200 million to put right. Improvements to the storm water drainage system would help reduce this risk in the future.

Opinion poll	
Which of these is the most important problem facing Rockford City at present?	
Environment	21%
Poor schools	26%
Flood defences	26%
Public transport	10%
Local economy/jobs	17%

Selected Economic Statistics for Rockford City		
	2000	**2003**
Average earnings	$25 750	$26 906
Unemployment	10%	7%
Average house price	$95 000	$110 000

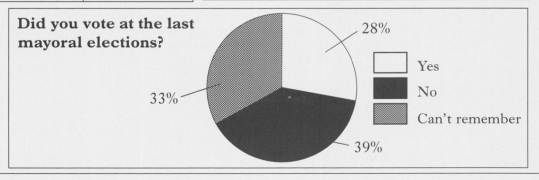

Did you vote at the last mayoral elections?

28% — Yes
39% — No
33% — Can't remember

QUESTION 3 (A) (*b*) (CONTINUED)

SOURCE 1

Profile of Brent Landon

Brent Landon has been mayor of Rockford City for the past 4 years. He qualified as a lawyer over 20 years ago, and has worked in the city ever since. As a result, he knows the community well and has used his legal knowledge to assist local charities.

Extracts from his campaign website:

- My first priority is the local economy. During my term in office, there have been more jobs created and higher pay. I want this to continue but not by building a new shopping complex. The city needs parks and open spaces where people can enjoy their leisure time.
- We can be proud of our local schools. However, I want only the best for our children and I will strive to make the changes to the education system that are necessary to bring children from all racial backgrounds together.
- The recent floods took us all by surprise. I will ensure that this city invests in flood prevention schemes to minimise the effect of future events.
- I will make public transport a big priority.
- I will expand the Voter Registration Programme to get more people involved in local politics.

SOURCE 2

Profile of Louise Crossan

Louise Crossan is a businesswoman who owns several retail outlets employing 35 local people. She moved to Rockford City 5 years ago and, although she has not held public office, she is a member of the local Chamber of Commerce.

Extracts from her campaign website:

- I want to see our community growing. I will work to attract new retail and leisure businesses to the city. This will help our local economy to continue its economic growth.
- The city has been spending too much which has resulted in local property taxes having to be increased. This is bad for business. I will balance the books even if it means postponing less important projects such as a new flood defence scheme.
- The condition of our streets is very poor. Regular maintenance must be improved. I will work to ensure the completion of improved highways to our neighbouring towns and cities.
- Education is vital. We must improve some of our older schools. I am for the creation of a magnet school in Rockford City even though it will involve large numbers of children having to travel to school.
- There is no point wasting money on Voter Registration Schemes—democracy already works well in Rockford City.

Using **only** the information about Rockford City and Sources 1 and 2 above, **explain which person would be the most suitable to be elected by the people of Rockford City as their new Mayor.**

Give **detailed** reasons to **explain your choice** and **why you rejected the other candidate**.

In your answer you **must** relate information about the city to the information about the two candidates.

(Enquiry Skills, **10** marks)

[NOW GO TO QUESTION 4 ON PAGE 23]

[BLANK PAGE]

QUESTION 3 (CONTINUED)

(B) **RUSSIA**

(*a*) | *Social and economic inequality has grown in Russia in recent years.* |

Explain, **in detail**, why *social and economic inequality* has grown in Russia in recent years.

In your answer you **must** use Russian examples.

(Knowledge and Understanding, **8** marks)

[Turn over

QUESTION 3 (B) (CONTINUED)

(b)   Study the information about the city of Izhevsk below. Also study the information in Sources 1 and 2 opposite. Sources 1 and 2 contain information about the two people who are candidates to become leader of the local Council for Izhevsk.

Information about Izhevsk

Izhevsk is the largest city in Udmurtia. The city is located in the Ural mountains to the east of Moscow. The population of Izhevsk is 700 000. The city is typical of many in Russia.

- Izhevsk lake is a popular place with local people. It has an inland beach where people can sunbathe and enjoy the water. Concerns have been growing recently about pollution with several bathers reporting mystery illnesses after bathing in the lake. There is speculation that this may be linked to the local zinc-processing industry.

- Izhevsk is an important car and lorry manufacturing centre. Car ownership has increased in recent years but the quality of the road system is very poor. Deep potholes cause damage to vehicles and during the rush hour there are frequent traffic jams. Dangerous driving leads to many accidents.

- There are three large armaments factories in Izhevsk. These produce guns, ammunition and other military equipment. The Russian government has been buying fewer weapons recently and this has led to cut-backs in the factory order books. Unemployment has been rising as workers lose their jobs.

- The University of Izhevsk used to be regarded as one of the best in the country. The Faculty of Engineering had a particularly good reputation. Lack of funds means that many university staff have now been paid off and the facilities badly need upgraded.

Opinion poll	
Which of these is the most important problem facing Izhevsk at present?	
Rising crime	23%
Poor schools	18%
Poor health services	14%
Dealing with Chechnya	9%
Corrupt politicians	36%

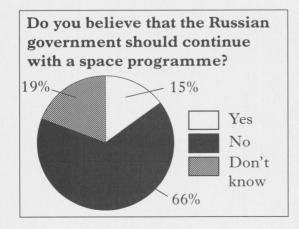

Do you believe that the Russian government should continue with a space programme?

19%   15%

Yes
No
Don't know

66%

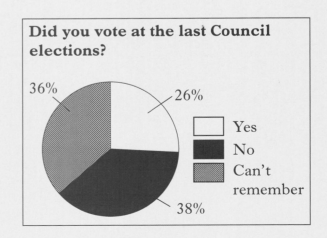

Did you vote at the last Council elections?

36%   26%

Yes
No
Can't remember

38%

QUESTION 3 (B) (*b*) (CONTINUED)

SOURCE 1

Profile of Vasili Kharine

51-year-old Vasili was born in Izhevsk. However, he has worked in other towns and cities nearby in recent years. When he was younger he played football for the local team. He has been involved in local government in a neighbouring city.

Extracts from his campaign leaflet:

- I am keenly interested in environmental issues. As a student I got into trouble with the authorities for trying to promote the activities of "Greenpeace".
- In my present role as Director of roads and traffic management, I have succeeded in reducing traffic congestion which has led to a decrease in serious accidents.
- Poor health services are of great concern to the voters. Improving them is my top priority.
- Russia needs a higher profile around the world. For that reason, we must continue with the space programme. Russia should be in the forefront of modern technology and science.
- I think it is terrible that some people in Izhevsk are frightened to leave their homes at night because of crime. Violence and robbery are on the increase—I will take steps to deal with this.

SOURCE 2

Profile of Dmitri Kulkov

52-year-old Dmitri was born in Izhevsk and has lived there for most of his life. He had a spell in the Armed Forces, rising to the rank of Captain. He was decorated for his bravery during the Afghan War in 1979. He has no previous involvement in politics.

Extracts from his campaign leaflet:

- There is no evidence that the people of Izhevsk are bored with politics. The turnout at recent elections has been very good.
- I believe that the Russian government should expand its armed forces. I believe that Russia needs the weapons to be a strong force in an unstable world.
- The decline of the University of Izhevsk has been bad for the city. I promise that there will be fresh investment to bring the university up to modern standards.
- Money that has been spent on Russia's ambitious space programme should be diverted to internal military threats. I also think that instead of sending cosmonauts into space we would be better dealing with the Chechens and any other terrorist threats.
- Some politicians have let the people down badly through their links with crime. They have taken bribes. I will deal strongly with corruption in government.

Using **only** the information about Izhevsk and Sources 1 and 2 above, **explain which person would be the most suitable to be elected by the people of Izhevsk as their new local Council leader.**

Give **detailed** reasons to **explain your choice** and **why you rejected the other candidate**.

In your answer you **must** relate information about the city to the information about the two candidates.

(Enquiry Skills, **10** marks)

[NOW GO TO QUESTION 4 ON PAGE 23]

[BLANK PAGE]

QUESTION 3 (CONTINUED)

(C) **CHINA**

(a)

> *Social and economic inequality has grown in China in recent years.*

Explain, **in detail**, why *social and economic inequality* has grown in China in recent years.

In your answer you **must** use Chinese examples.

(Knowledge and Understanding, **8** marks)

[Turn over

QUESTION 3 (C) (CONTINUED)

(b)   Study the information about the village of Sanbu below. Also study the information in Sources 1 and 2 opposite. Sources 1 and 2 contain information about the two people who are candidates to become head of the village Committee in Sanbu.

Information about Sanbu

Sanbu is a village in Central China. It is 30 miles from the nearest large town. It has a population of 19 000.

- Agriculture has been an important part of the economy of Sanbu. Many farmers have taken advantage of the changes in agricultural policy to expand their businesses and now want more access to the markets in nearby towns. To do this, they need better roads and transport facilities. Many resent previous spending on projects like a pig-raising project forced on them by a decision taken by the Communist Party in Beijing and want to make their own decisions on investment.

- The major industry in Sanbu is a factory which strips down parts from old American computers and mobile phones. This employs 120 people and the local Communist Party is keen to see this expand to stop the drift to the towns of young people seeking better employment opportunities. This factory releases toxic chemicals like mercury and dioxins into the air and water. There is suspicion that this is the cause of rising cancer cases in local school children.

- Drug addiction is a growing health problem in Sanbu. The village is on a new drug trail from central China to the cities in the south. Many of the younger villagers have become drug addicts. Their parents are desperate for more help for their children to combat the problem and also the threat of AIDS.

Opinion poll	
Which of these is the most important problem facing Sanbu at present?	
Poor access to markets	29%
Poor water supply	4%
Creating industrial jobs	26%
Poor health services	16%
Education	25%

Do you think that democracy should be extended in China?	
Yes	59%
No	34%
Don't know	7%

Do you agree with the Communist Party that drug addicts should be severely punished?

8%   69%

23%

☐ Yes
■ No
▨ Don't know

QUESTION 3 (C) (*b*) (CONTINUED)

SOURCE 1

Profile of Fang Zhizhen

Fang is 53 years old and has been a member of the Communist Party for 35 years. He is married with one son in accordance with the One Child Policy. He was educated locally and has only left the village for Party rallies. The local Communist Party has nominated Fang to continue in his post as head of the village Committee. Fang has been involved in local government for many years.

Extracts from his campaign poster:

- I support fully all the policies of the Communist Party and believe that few people in China want more democracy.

- I am proud that the Communist Party was responsible for bringing many computer jobs to the village and believe that the future economy of Sanbu lies in expanding industry.

- I am a firm believer in the Communist Party policy of a tough line on drugs. I believe that the only way to tackle the problem of drug addiction is to have tough penalties on users. The party is right to use severe punishments for this crime.

- One of my main aims for the future is to ensure that conditions for people in Sanbu improve. I have plans to improve the water and sewage as well as ensuring that the school is provided with more resources and a better building.

SOURCE 2

Profile of Qumo Aqu

Qumo was born in Beijing and educated at Beijing University. She spent a year in the USA studying medicine. After her marriage, she came to practise as a doctor in Sanbu. She has two children, one boy and one girl and is glad that the Communist Party has adopted a new policy of "One-Son-Two-Children". She is not a member of the Communist Party and believes that people should have a bigger choice in who runs their village Committee.

Extracts from her campaign poster:

- I believe that local farmers should be supported as more people depend on agriculture than industry. I am of the opinion that better roads would make it easier to get products to markets.

- I am opposed to industries like the computer industry which damage our environment and affect the health of our children.

- As a doctor, I see the effects of the drug problem but believe that addicts need help rather than punishment. Addicts need acupuncture and herbal medicine as well as counselling. This is a better way to deal with the problem.

- Money should be spent on education and improvements in the water supply. If people were able to decide for themselves what taxes should be spent on, this would ensure that the needs of the village were met and people would be more willing to pay.

Using **only** the information about Sanbu and Sources 1 and 2 above, **explain which person would be the most suitable to be elected by the people of Sanbu as their head of the village Committee.**

Give **detailed** reasons to **explain your choice** and **why you rejected the other candidate**.

In your answer you **must** relate information about the village to the information about the two candidates.

(Enquiry Skills, **10** marks)

[NOW GO TO QUESTION 4 ON PAGE 23]

[BLANK PAGE]

SYLLABUS AREA 4—INTERNATIONAL RELATIONS

QUESTION 4

(a)

> *Wealthy countries have had economic power over African countries in recent years.*

Describe, **in detail**, the ways in which wealthy countries from outside Africa have used their **economic power** in their relations with less well-off African countries in recent years.

(Knowledge and Understanding, **4** marks)

(b)

> *The aid policies of the United Nations have helped meet the needs of some African countries.*

Describe, **in detail**, the ways in which the *aid policies of the United Nations have helped meet the* **needs** *of some African countries.*

(Knowledge and Understanding, **4** marks)

[Turn over

QUESTION 4 (CONTINUED)

You have been asked to carry out **two** investigations.

The first investigation is on the topic in the box below.

> **The European Union (EU) in the 21st Century.**

Now answer questions (*c*) and (*d*) which follow.

(*c*)   State a relevant **hypothesis** for your investigation.

(Enquiry Skills, **2** marks)

(*d*)   Give **two** relevant **aims** to help you prove or disprove your hypothesis.

(Enquiry Skills, **2** marks)

The second investigation is on the topic in the box below.

> **The North Atlantic Treaty Organisation (NATO) in the 21st Century.**

Now answer questions (*e*) and (*f*) which follow.

Your class decides to carry out a survey of public opinion about NATO.

(*e*)   Describe, **in detail**, **two** factors that must be taken into account when designing and carrying out a survey.

(Enquiry Skills, **4** marks)

QUESTION 4 (CONTINUED)

(*f*)   You also decide to carry out a search on the Internet.

You enter the phrase, "NATO in the 21st Century", into the BBC news website search engine.

Six results are shown below.

Which result do you think would be the **most useful**? **Explain** your answer.

(Enquiry Skills, **2** marks)

[END OF QUESTION PAPER]

[BLANK PAGE]

[BLANK PAGE]

G

2640/402

NATIONAL   MONDAY, 22 MAY   MODERN STUDIES
QUALIFICATIONS   10.20 AM–11.50 AM   STANDARD GRADE
2006   General Level

1   Read every question carefully.

2   Answer all questions as fully as you can.

3   If you cannot do a question, go on to the next one. Try again later.

4   In question 3, answer **one** section only; Section (A) The USA **or** Section (B) Russia **or** Section (C) China.

5   Write your answers in the answer book provided. Indicate clearly, in the left hand margin, the question and section of question being answered. Do not write in the right hand margin.

SCOTTISH
QUALIFICATIONS
AUTHORITY

©

SYLLABUS AREA 1—LIVING IN A DEMOCRACY

QUESTION 1

(a)

> *Trade union members have rights and responsibilities.*

Describe **one** right and **one** responsibility that a trade union member has.

(Knowledge & Understanding, **4** marks)

(b) Study Sources 1 and 2 below, then answer the question which follows.

SOURCE 1

Workers who are Trade Union Members (%)		
Year	*Male*	*Female*
1999	27·3	27·1
2001	26·6	27·1
2003	25·5	27·2

SOURCE 2

Trade Union Membership in Different Jobs (%)				
Type of Job	*1998*		*2002*	
	Males	*Females*	*Males*	*Females*
Managers and Administrators	18	21	16	22
Secretarial	30	22	31	23
Sales and Customer Services	18	12	13	13

Write down **two** conclusions about the membership of trade unions.

You must **only** use the information above.

You should write **one** conclusion about **each** of the following.

- Changes in male **or** female trade union membership between 1999 and 2003

- Changes in male **and** female trade union membership **in one of the jobs** between 1998 and 2002

(Enquiry Skills, **4** marks)

QUESTION 1 (CONTINUED)

(*c*) Study the information below, then answer the question which follows.

> ### TRADE UNIONS AND THE SCOTTISH LABOUR PARTY
>
> • Labour has the largest number of MSPs in the Scottish Parliament.
>
> • A committee of the Labour Party in Scotland, which has trade union representatives on it, writes policies on which the Labour Party fights elections.
>
> • Some trade unions give money to and campaign for Labour Party candidates in elections.
>
> • Many MSPs who were elected at the 2003 election were not members of trade unions.
>
> • A quarter of a million Scottish voters are members of trade unions.
>
> • Trade unionists do not need to vote for the Labour Party in Scotland.

> Trade unions play an important part in the election of Labour MSPs. Trade unions also play a part in policy making for the Labour Party.

View of Anne Hall

Give **two** reasons to **support** the view of Anne Hall.

(Enquiry Skills, **4** marks)

(*d*) | *Local councillors and MSPs are representatives who work on behalf of people in their area.* |

Choose **ONE** of the following representatives:

• local councillors

• MSPs.

Describe **two** ways in which *the representative you have chosen works on behalf of people in their area.*

(Knowledge & Understanding, **4** marks)

[Turn over

SYLLABUS AREA 2—CHANGING SOCIETY

QUESTION 2

(a) | Many elderly people live in their own homes. Some of these homes have been adapted to meet their needs.

Give **two ways** in which homes can be adapted to meet the needs of some elderly people.

For **each** way, explain how it meets their needs.

(Knowledge & Understanding, **4** marks)

(b) Study Sources 1 and 2 below, then answer the question which follows.

SOURCE 1

Goodbye Geriatrics – Hello Geri-actives

Older people today have decided to become "Geri-actives" in their retirement. They want to enjoy new experiences. What these "Geri-actives" plan to do in retirement varies greatly. Their top six plans for "life after work" are gardening (60%), meeting friends (58%), travelling (57%), painting (14%), golf (11%) and writing novels (9%). Paying for these new activities may cost a lot of money. Arranging to have a good pension and saving as much as possible are essential for people nearing retirement.

SOURCE 2

The Percentage of Grandmothers who . . .

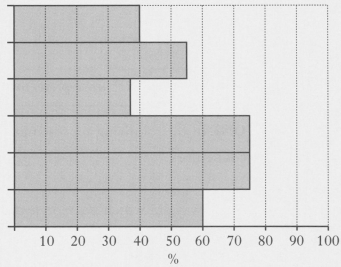

. . . look after grandchildren every week.

. . . have a home computer.

. . . send regular text messages.

. . . have a mobile phone.

. . . go to coffee bars.

. . . own a car.

There are more elderly people today than ever before. Most grandmothers use very little technology. When most people retire, they just want to meet friends, travel and play golf. Elderly people should have a good pension.

View of Dennis Baxter

Using **only** Sources 1 and 2 above, write down **two** statements made by Dennis Baxter that are **exaggerated**.

Using the information in the Sources, give **one** reason why **each** of the statements you have chosen is **exaggerated**.

(Enquiry Skills, **4** marks)

QUESTION 2 (CONTINUED)

You are investigating the topic in the box below.

> **Local groups that help the elderly.**

Answer questions (*c*), (*d*), (*e*) and (*f*) which follow.

(*c*)   As part of the **Planning Stage**, give **two** relevant aims for your investigation.

(Enquiry Skills, **2** marks)

You decide to collect information about **local groups that help the elderly**.

(*d*)   Give **two** relevant **ways** to gather information to help in your investigation.

(Enquiry Skills, **2** marks)

(*e*)   For **one** of these ways, explain why it is a **good** way to get information to help in your investigation.

(Enquiry Skills, **2** marks)

You have been asked to develop your investigation. You decide to find out about a **national organisation** which helps the elderly.

You see the following advert in a newspaper.

Study the advert carefully, then answer the question which follows.

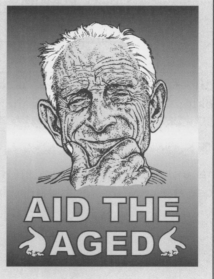

AID THE AGED
National Roadshow

Fridays in June from **10 am–2 pm**

Coming to various venues around Scotland.
Watch the national press for more details.

If you are over 55 – come along and learn how
we can help you.

Come along early and bring
a friend!

Advice and help given to all.
No problem too big or too small.

AID THE AGED

(*f*)   You decide to visit the Aid The Aged National Roadshow to collect more information to help in your investigation.

Using **only** the information in the advert above, give **one difficulty** you might have in visiting this roadshow.

(Enquiry Skills, **2** marks)

SYLLABUS AREA 3—IDEOLOGIES

QUESTION 3

Answer **ONE** section only: Section (A)—The USA on pages *six* to *eight*

OR Section (B)—Russia on pages *nine* to *eleven*

OR Section (C)—China on pages *twelve* to *fourteen*

(A) **THE USA**

(*a*)

> *The American people can use the media to criticise the government.*

Describe **two** ways that *the American people can use the media to criticise the government.*

In your answer you **must** use American examples.

(Knowledge & Understanding, **4** marks)

(*b*)   Study the information below, then answer the question which follows.

Cigarette Smoking amongst selected Groups in the USA (%)

	1990	2001
All Males	28·0	24·7
White Males	27·6	24·9
Black Males	32·8	27·6
All Females	22·9	20·8
White Females	23·5	22·1
Black Females	20·8	17·9
US Average	25·3	22·7

> In the USA, men are less likely to smoke than women. The smallest drop in smoking has been amongst white females.

View of Nancy Holstein

Using **only** the information above, give **one** reason to **support** and **one** reason to **oppose** the view of Nancy Holstein.

(Enquiry Skills, **4** marks)

QUESTION 3 (A) (CONTINUED)

(*c*)

> *In recent years, many members of ethnic minority groups in the USA have seen an improvement in their standards of living.*

Give **two** reasons to explain why *many members of ethnic minority groups in the USA have seen an improvement in their standards of living.*

In your answer you **must** use American examples.

(Knowledge & Understanding, **4** marks)

[Turn over

QUESTION 3 (A) (CONTINUED)

(d)   Study the Timeline below, then answer the question which follows.

TIMELINE – WAR ON TERROR

KEY EVENTS 2001–2005

Date	Event
September 11 2001	Nearly 3000 people are killed when 2 airliners are hijacked by Al Qaeda terrorists and are crashed into the World Trade Centre in New York.
October 2001	American and allied troops invade Afghanistan to remove the Taliban government and destroy Al Qaeda forces in that country.
February 2003	Khalid Mohammed, a suspected terrorist and chief planner of the September 11 attacks, is captured in Pakistan.
March 2003	Thousands of US troops and their allies invade Iraq to remove the government of Saddam Hussein. He is accused of helping terrorist groups and of making weapons of mass destruction.
December 2003	Saddam Hussein is captured near Baghdad. It is expected that he will be charged with many crimes.
July 2005	Terrorist bombs explode on a bus and on a number of underground passenger trains in the city of London. Many people are killed and injured.

Since September 11 2001, US troops have only invaded one country. In that time terrorists have killed more innocent people. America is the only country to suffer from terrorist attacks. Some important people have been captured in the war against terror.

Statements by an American Journalist

Using **only** the information above, write down **two** statements made by the American Journalist which are **exaggerated**.

Using the Timeline, give **one** reason why **each** of the statements you have chosen is **exaggerated**.

(Enquiry Skills, **4** marks)

NOW GO TO QUESTION 4 ON PAGE FIFTEEN

QUESTION 3 (CONTINUED)

(B) **RUSSIA**

(a) | *The Russian people can use the media to criticise the government.* |

Describe **two** ways that *the Russian people can use the media to criticise the government.*
In your answer you **must** use Russian examples.

(Knowledge & Understanding, **4** marks)

(b) Study the information below, then answer the question which follows.

Salaries of People in selected Occupations in Russia

Average Salary (US Dollars)			
Occupation	*2002*	*2003*	*% Change*
Financial Controller	500	650	+30
IT Company Director	3000	4500	+50
Lawyer	1750	2100	+20
Personnel Director	1250	2000	+60
Sales Manager	400	900	+125
Secretary	300	325	+8
Training Manager	750	1050	+40

| Jobs in IT and the Law have the highest salaries. These jobs have also seen the biggest change in salaries between 2002 and 2003. |

View of Natalia Medvedev

Using **only** the information above, give **one** reason to **support** and **one** reason to **oppose** the view of Natalia Medvedev.

(Enquiry Skills, **4** marks)

[Turn over

QUESTION 3 (B) (CONTINUED)

(*c*)

> *People living in the major cities tend to have a better standard of living than those living in other parts of Russia.*

Give **two** reasons why *people living in the major cities tend to have a better standard of living than those living in other parts of Russia.*

In your answer you **must** use Russian examples.

(Knowledge & Understanding, **4** marks)

QUESTION 3 (B) (CONTINUED)

(*d*)   Study the Timeline below, then answer the question which follows.

TIMELINE – CHECHNYA

KEY EVENTS 2000–2004

Date	Event
May 2000	President Putin of Russia declares that Chechnya will be ruled directly from Moscow. He is determined to defeat the Chechen rebels by all means available to him.
November 2001	Official talks take place between Russian authorities and Chechen rebels on a possible peace settlement. Talks break up without agreement.
December 2001	A captured rebel Chechen army commander is sentenced to life imprisonment by a court in Moscow.
October 2002	Chechen rebels seize a theatre in Moscow, the Russian capital, and hold 800 people hostage. 120 hostages are killed by the rebels when Russian forces storm the building. Most of the rebels are then killed by the Russian troops in the battle which follows.
March 2003	Russian people are pleased with the result of the ballot in Chechnya which shows a majority of Chechens in favour of remaining part of Russia.
May 2004	Recently elected President of Chechnya, Akhmad Kadyrov, killed in a bomb blast carried out by Chechen rebels.

> It is the Chechen rebels who have carried out all the killings. Elections have taken place in Chechnya. Important politicians on both sides have been directly involved in the war. A settlement between the two sides is within reach.

Statements by a Russian Journalist

Using **only** the information above, write down **two** statements made by the Russian Journalist, which are **exaggerated**.

Using the Timeline, give **one** reason why **each** of the statements you have chosen is **exaggerated**.

(Enquiry Skills, 4 marks)

NOW GO TO QUESTION 4 ON PAGE FIFTEEN

QUESTION 3 (CONTINUED)

(C) CHINA

(*a*)

> *The Chinese people are not allowed to criticise the government.*

Describe **two** actions which the Chinese Government might take to deal with those who do criticise the government.

In your answer you **must** use Chinese examples.

(Knowledge & Understanding, **4** marks)

(*b*) Study the information below, then answer the question which follows.

Population with Internet Access in selected Countries (%)			
Country	*2003*	*2004*	*2005*
China	8	10	25
USA	43	47	54
Russia	15	17	24
Japan	48	51	53
UK	40	42	46

> China has always had the lowest Internet access of all the world's major countries. However, it is showing the fastest growth.

View of Li Tie

Using **only** the information above, give **one** reason to **support** and **one** reason to **oppose** the view of Li Tie.

(Enquiry Skills, **4** marks)

QUESTION 3 (C) (CONTINUED)

(c)

> *People living in the major cities tend to have a better standard of living than those living in other parts of China.*

Give **two** reasons why *people living in the major cities tend to have a better standard of living than those living in other parts of China.*

In your answer you **must** use Chinese examples.

(Knowledge & Understanding, **4** marks)

[Turn over

QUESTION 3 (C) (CONTINUED)

(d) Study the Timeline below, then answer the question which follows.

TIMELINE – THE THREE GORGES DAM PROJECT

KEY EVENTS 1992–2009

Date	Event
1992	Work starts on the dam. The project is expected to take 17 years to complete and will open in 2009.
February 1993	20 000 people start work around the clock on the dam. 250 000 people will have had jobs building the dam by the time it is finished.
July 1993	Journalist Dai Qing is jailed for ten months for criticising the project. Over the next year, hundreds of others are also jailed by the Chinese government.
1999	The government begins an inquiry into safety at the site after 40 workers are killed in an accident.
2003	The Chinese government claims that only 1·2 million people will lose their homes when the valley is flooded. Some people claim it will be 2 million.
2009	Over 100 million people will have electricity for the first time when the dam is finished.

The Three Gorges Dam is a huge building project. Every Chinese person will benefit when the project is finished. Electricity will improve the lives of many Chinese people. Everyone in China supports the project.

Statements by a Chinese Journalist

Using **only** the information above, write down **two** statements made by the Chinese Journalist which are **exaggerated**.

Using the Timeline, give **one** reason why **each** of the statements you have chosen is **exaggerated**.

(Enquiry Skills, **4** marks)

NOW GO TO QUESTION 4 ON PAGE FIFTEEN

SYLLABUS AREA 4—INTERNATIONAL RELATIONS

QUESTION 4

(*a*) **United Nations Specialised Agencies**

Food and Agricultural
Organisation

United Nations
Children's Fund

World Health
Organisation

Choose **one** of the UN Specialised Agencies above.

Describe **two** ways in which the agency you have chosen tries to meet the **needs** of people in Africa.

(Knowledge & Understanding, **4** marks)

(*b*) Study Sources 1 and 2 below, then answer the question which follows.

SOURCE 1	**SOURCE 2**
United Nations Press Release	**Sudanese Government Press Release**
A large number of people have been forced to leave their homes and over 50 000 have been killed in the Darfur region of Sudan since 2003. Darfur itself is a very dry area in the west of Sudan, the largest country in Africa. There has been conflict between black Africans and Arabs in the region for many years. Due to this there is a lack of aid and children are now dying of hunger.	Darfur is a desert area in the west of the largest country in Africa, Sudan. It is well known that there is fighting between the Arabs and black Africans in Darfur which has caused many deaths. Our country needs more money to be able to develop. However, everybody has enough to eat. A large number of people have chosen to leave their homes in Darfur and move to other countries such as Chad.

Sources 1 and 2 give different views about **what has been happening in the Darfur region of Sudan**.

Write down **two** differences between these views.

You **must** only use information from the Sources above.

(Enquiry Skills, **4** marks)

[Turn over for Questions 4(*c*) and 4(*d*) on *Page sixteen*

QUESTION 4 (CONTINUED)

(c)

TIED AID – SOME FACTS
• Tied aid cuts the value of aid by 25–40%. • The United Kingdom is one of only four countries stopping tied aid. • 60–75% of Canadian aid is tied. • The USA, Germany, Japan and France still insist on most of their aid being "tied". • The USA makes sure that 80c in every dollar is returned to the USA. • The USA insists that anti-AIDS drugs are bought from the USA instead of cheaper products from South Africa, India or Brazil.

Give **two** reasons why some rich countries give tied aid to countries in Africa.

(Knowledge & Understanding, **4** marks)

(d) Study the information below, then answer the question which follows.

Selected Statistics for three African Countries in 2004			
	Benin	Kenya	Nigeria
Infant deaths (per 1000 live births)	85	62	70
Life expectancy (years)	51	45	50
HIV/AIDS in adult population (%)	1·9	6·7	5·4
Population below poverty line (%)	37	50	60
Literacy rate (%)	41	85	68
Voting age (years)	18	18	18

Statements made by Alison Grey, Aid Worker
• Benin has a smaller percentage of its population living in poverty than either Kenya or Nigeria. • Nigeria has the highest rate of HIV/AIDS amongst adults. • Infant deaths are lowest in Benin. • The literacy rate in all three countries is very similar. • Life expectancy is lowest in Kenya.

Using **only** the information above, write down **two** statements made by Alison Grey which are **correct**.

Using the information, give **one** reason why **each** of the statements you have chosen is **correct**.

(Enquiry Skills, **4** marks)

[END OF QUESTION PAPER]

[BLANK PAGE]

C

2640/403

NATIONAL
QUALIFICATIONS
2006

MONDAY, 22 MAY
1.00 PM – 3.00 PM

MODERN STUDIES
STANDARD GRADE
Credit Level

1 Read every question carefully.

2 Answer all questions as fully as you can.

3 If you cannot do a question, go on to the next one. Try again later.

4 In question 3, answer **one** section only: Section (A) The USA **or** Section (B) Russia **or** Section (C) China.

5 Write your answers in the answer book provided. Indicate clearly, in the left hand margin, the question and section of question being answered. Do not write in the right hand margin.

SCOTTISH
QUALIFICATIONS
AUTHORITY

©

SYLLABUS AREA 1—LIVING IN A DEMOCRACY

QUESTION 1

(a) | *Candidates rely on help from party workers and volunteers during election campaigns.* |

Describe, **in detail**, the ways in which party workers and volunteers can help during election campaigns.

(Knowledge & Understanding, **6** marks)

(b) | *In a democracy, it is important that people use their right to vote.* |

Explain, **in detail,** why it is important for people to use their **right** to vote.

(Knowledge & Understanding, **4** marks)

You have been asked to carry out **two** investigations.

The first investigation is on the topic in the box below.

| **Voting systems used in elections in Scotland.** |

Now answer questions (c) and (d) which follow.

(c) State a relevant **hypothesis** for your investigation.

(Enquiry Skills, **2** marks)

(d) Give **two** relevant **aims** to help you prove or disprove your hypothesis.

(Enquiry Skills, **2** marks)

QUESTION 1 (CONTINUED)

The second investigation is on the topic in the box below.

> Peoples' attitude towards voting.

Now answer questions (e) and (f) which follow.

(e)   While collecting information for your investigation, you find the following survey result.

Question: Can people influence political decisions by voting?	
Age	% saying yes
16–19	17
20–29	26
30–39	25
40–49	27
50–64	25
65+	22
Source: Home Office Citizenship Survey: (Statistics Directorate), September 2004 [based on 9600 replies, UK wide]	

Give **two** detailed reasons why the above survey is a **good** source of information to use in your investigation.

(Enquiry Skills, **4** marks)

(f)   You then decide to collect more information by carrying out your own survey about peoples' attitude to voting in your local area.

Give **one other relevant** question which you could include in your survey.

(Enquiry Skills, **2** marks)

[Turn over

SYLLABUS AREA 2—CHANGING SOCIETY

QUESTION 2

(*a*)
Recent Government Policies to improve Employment Opportunities

 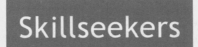 

Choose **two** policies from the list above.

Describe, **in detail**, the ways in which each policy has tried to improve employment opportunities.

(Knowledge & Understanding, **6** marks)

QUESTION 2 (CONTINUED)

(b) Study Sources 1 and 2 below, then answer the question which follows.

SOURCE 1

Households by type in Scotland, 1981–2003 (%)			
	1981	**1991**	**2003**
Single Adult	7·2	12·9	15·9
Pensioner (single or couple)	28·9	29·8	30·8
Couple no children	28·4	27·1	26·7
Single Parent with children	2·3	4·9	5·8
Couple with children	33·2	25·3	20·8

SOURCE 2

Selected Scottish households living in poverty (%)

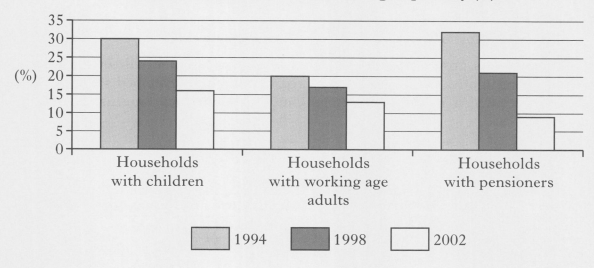

Households consisting of pensioners have grown the most in percentage terms. However, they have experienced less of an improvement in the quality of their lives than other groups.

View of Sandy Mathieson

Give **two** reasons to **oppose** the view of Sandy Mathieson.

(Enquiry Skills, **4** marks)

[Turn over

QUESTION 2 (CONTINUED)

(c)   Study Sources 1, 2, 3 and 4 below and opposite, then answer the question which follows.

SOURCE 1

Scotland – a country in industrial change

The traditional male dominated production and construction industries in Scotland are all in decline. In 2000, Scotland only had 35 000 working in oil, gas and fishing, traditionally some of Scotland's key industries. The new growth industries in Scotland are all service industries such as call centres, Biotechnology, Software and e-Business.

A new service industry which has grown in Scotland is call centres. In 1998, Scotland's call centre industry employed 16 000 workers, of which 42% were women. By 2000, this figure had grown to 37 000. Five years on, there are 60 000 people employed in them. Considerable growth is predicted in the industry and of the 290 call centres, 92 predict increased employment by 2007. Around 67% of Scottish call centre staff is now female. 75% of the staff is under 35 and about 33% of the staff is part-time. Most of these part-time workers are female.

Much of this growth in the new service industries can be directly attributed to a stable and motivated Scottish workforce with highly developed skills. It is also a workforce which is now willing to have more flexible work patterns than traditionally was the case.

SOURCE 2

The Scottish Workforce (figures in thousands)	Males		Females	
	1998	2002	1998	2002
Agriculture, Forestry and Fishing	31	29	8	8
Production and Construction Industries				
Construction	113	108	24	14
Energy and Water	37	32	9	9
Manufacturing	227	189	99	74
Service Industries				
Banking, Finance and Insurance	156	187	170	191
Distribution, Hotels and Catering, Repairs	214	238	289	308
Public Administration, Education and Health	163	176	394	458
Transport and Communication	86	93	28	32
Other Services	52	62	54	63
Total employed	**1079**	**1114**	**1075**	**1157**

QUESTION 2(c) (CONTINUED)

SOURCE 3

Working conditions – Number of part-time workers in Scotland (000s)

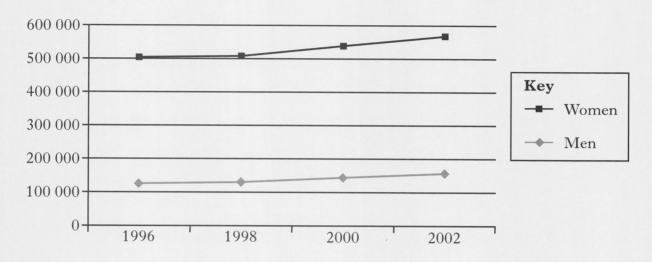

SOURCE 4

Working conditions – Female earnings as a percentage (%) of male earnings

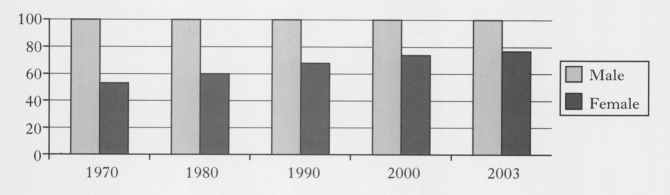

> Women are becoming more important to the Scottish economy in the 21st century. Furthermore, this is reflected in the changes in their pay and conditions.

View of Tom Anderson

Using **only** Sources 1, 2, 3 and 4, explain **the extent to which** Tom Anderson could be accused of being **selective in the use of facts**.

(Enquiry Skills, **8** marks)

[Turn over

[BLANK PAGE]

SYLLABUS AREA 3—IDEOLOGIES

QUESTION 3

Answer **one** section only: Section (A)—The USA on pages *nine* to *eleven*
OR Section (B)—Russia on pages *thirteen* to *fifteen*
OR Section (C)—China on pages *seventeen* to *nineteen*

(A) **THE USA**

(a) | *In the USA, citizens have both political rights and the responsibilities that go with them.* |

Describe, **in detail**, the **political rights** of American citizens and the **responsibilities** that go with them.

In your answer you **must** use American examples.

(Knowledge and Understanding, **8** marks)

[Turn over

QUESTION 3 (A) (CONTINUED)

(b) Study Sources 1, 2, 3 and 4 and the information on New York City, then answer the question which follows.

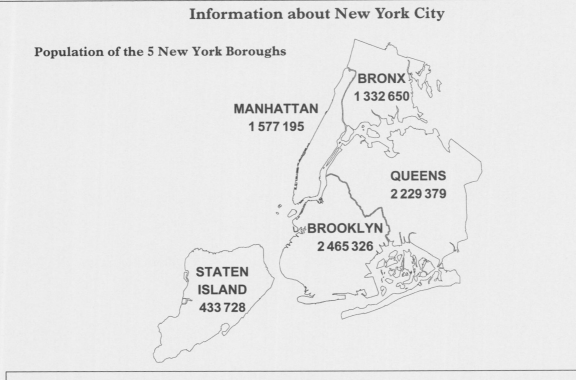

Information about New York City

Population of the 5 New York Boroughs

BRONX
1 332 650

MANHATTAN
1 577 195

QUEENS
2 229 379

BROOKLYN
2 465 326

STATEN
ISLAND
433 728

New York has a population of 8 008 278, which makes it America's largest city.
It has experienced a 10% increase in its population since 1990.
It is a city with a great mix of different races, nationalities and cultures.
The city is itself divided into five Boroughs: The Bronx, Brooklyn, Manhattan, Queens and Staten Island.

Racial Composition of Population in New York City		
White	2 801 267	35·0%
Hispanic	2 160 554	27·0%
Black	1 962 154	24·5%
Asian/Pacific Islanders	783 058	9·8%
Native Americans	17 321	0·2%
Other	283 924	3·5%

SOURCE 1

New York Boroughs: Population in 2000 by Race (%)

	Bronx	Brooklyn	Manhattan	Queens	Staten Island
White	14·5	34·6	45·8	32·9	71·3
Hispanic	48·4	19·8	27·2	25·0	12·1
Black	31·2	34·4	15·3	19·0	8·9
Asian/Pacific Islanders	2·9	7·5	9·4	17·5	5·6
Native Americans	0·3	0·2	0·2	0·3	0·1
Others	2·7	3·5	2·1	5·3	2·0

QUESTION 3 (A) (*b*) (CONTINUED)

SOURCE 2

New York Boroughs: Educational Attainment in 2000 by those aged 25+ (%)

	Did not complete High School	College Graduate
Bronx	38	15
Brooklyn	31	22
Manhattan	21	49
Queens	26	24
Staten Island	17	23

SOURCE 3

New York Boroughs: Crime Rate in 2000 (per 100 000 people)

	Person Crime	Property Crime	Total
Bronx	1112	2369	3481
Brooklyn	1024	2134	3158
Manhattan	895	3822	4717
Queens	583	2079	2662
Staten Island	332	1400	1732

SOURCE 4

New York Boroughs: Family Finances and Poverty Statistics in 2000

	Average Household Income ($)	Families in Poverty (%)
Bronx	28 000	27
Brooklyn	32 000	22
Manhattan	48 000	18
Queens	42 000	12
Staten Island	55 000	8

Using **only** the information about New York City and Sources 1, 2, 3, 4 above and opposite, what **conclusions** can be drawn about the ways in which the Boroughs are different from each other, and from the city as a whole?

You must **make** and **justify** a conclusion about **each** of the following headings.

- The Borough whose racial composition is **least** like that of the city as a whole
- The relationship between person crime rates and educational attainment
- The relationship between race and family finances
- The desirability of Manhattan as a Borough to live in

(Enquiry Skills, **8** marks)

[NOW GO TO QUESTION 4 ON PAGE 21]

[BLANK PAGE]

QUESTION 3 (CONTINUED)

(B) **RUSSIA**

(a) | *In Russia, citizens have both political rights and the responsibilities that go with them.* |

Describe, **in detail**, the ***political rights*** of Russian citizens and the ***responsibilities*** *that go with them.*

In your answer, you **must** use Russian examples.

(Knowledge and Understanding, **8** marks)

[Turn over

QUESTION 3 (B) (CONTINUED)

(b)   Study Sources 1, 2, 3 and 4 and the information on Russia, then answer the question which follows.

Information about Russia

Russia is the biggest country in Asia with a total population of 144 million and a labour force of 72 million. It has large deposits of coal, natural gas, oil and many other valuable minerals. Russia is one of the major economic powers in the world. Its economy has grown fast since the end of Communist rule in 1991. It earns billions of dollars from oil and petrol exports and has a total GDP of $1282 billion. Russia relies on trade with several neighbouring countries and it sells over 16% of its exports to, and buys 19% of its imports from, just five of its neighbours.

Russia and its neighbours

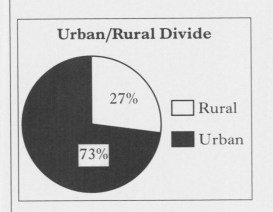

Urban/Rural Divide

Economic Information		
Sector	Employment (%)	Contribution to Wealth of Country (%)
Agriculture	12	5
Industry	24	35
Services	64	60

SOURCE 1

Selected Countries: Trade with Russia (%)

	Imports from Russia	Exports to Russia
Japan	1·7	3·1
Mongolia	33·9	6·5
Kazakhstan	34·9	15·5
Norway	2·4	2·5
North Korea	2·1	8·1

QUESTION 3 (B) (b) (CONTINUED)

SOURCE 2

Urban/Rural Divide in some of Russia's neighbours (%)

	Urban	Rural
Japan	79	21
Mongolia	57	43
Kazakhstan	56	44
Norway	75	25
North Korea	61	39

SOURCE 3

Employment in different sectors of the economy for some of Russia's neighbours (%)

	Agriculture	Industry	Services
Japan	5	25	70
Mongolia	79	6	15
Kazakhstan	20	30	50
Norway	4	22	74
North Korea	36	48	16

SOURCE 4

Contribution of each sector to the GDP for some of Russia's neighbours (%)

	Agriculture	Industry	Services
Japan	1	26	73
Mongolia	20	21	59
Kazakhstan	8	37	55
Norway	2	36	62
North Korea	30	34	36

Using **only** the information on Russia and Sources 1, 2, 3, 4 above and opposite, what **conclusions** can be drawn about the relationship between **Russia and her neighbours**?

You must **make** and **justify** a conclusion about **each** of the following headings.

- The urban/rural divide in Russia compared with some of her neighbours
- The relationship between the urban/rural divide and employment in agriculture
- The relationship between employment in services and their contribution to GDP
- The importance of Russia to the economies of the neighbouring countries

(Enquiry Skills, **8** marks)

[NOW GO TO QUESTION 4 ON PAGE 21]

[BLANK PAGE]

QUESTION 3 (CONTINUED)

(C) **CHINA**

(a)
> *The Communist government in China gives citizens certain rights. In return, citizens are expected to accept their responsibilities.*

Describe, **in detail**, the *rights* that Chinese citizens have and the *responsibilities* that go with them.

In your answer, you **must** use Chinese examples.

(Knowledge and Understanding, **8** marks)

[Turn over

QUESTION 3 (C) (CONTINUED)

(*b*)   Study Sources 1, 2, 3 and 4 and the information on China, then answer the question which follows.

Information about China

China is the second biggest country in Asia with a total population of 1·3 billion and a labour force of 744 million. It has large deposits of coal, natural gas, oil and many other valuable minerals. The government in China has turned the country into the major economic power in the region with the fastest growing economy in the world. China relies on trade with several countries in the region and has a total GDP of $6449 billion. It sells almost 21% of its exports to, and buys 25% of its imports from, just five of its neighbours.

China and its neighbours

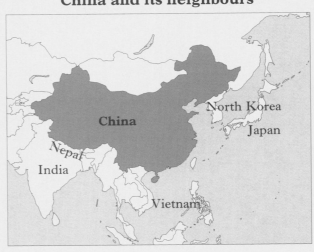

Urban/Rural Divide

37% Urban
63% Rural

Economic Information

Sector	Employment (%)	Contribution to wealth of country (%)
Agriculture	50	15
Industry	22	53
Services	28	32

SOURCE 1

Selected Countries: Trade with China (%)

	Imports from China	Exports to China
Japan	19·7	12·1
India	4·5	6·3
Vietnam	13·6	6·2
Nepal	13·5	0·5
North Korea	39·7	28·4

QUESTION 3 (C) (b) (CONTINUED)

SOURCE 2

Urban/Rural Divide in some of China's neighbours (%)

	Urban	Rural
Japan	79	21
India	28	72
Vietnam	25	75
Nepal	12	88
North Korea	61	39

SOURCE 3

Employment in different sectors of the economy for some of China's neighbours (%)

	Agriculture	Industry	Services
Japan	5	25	70
India	60	17	23
Vietnam	63	23	14
Nepal	81	3	16
North Korea	36	48	16

SOURCE 4

Contribution of each sector to the GDP for some of China's neighbours (%)

	Agriculture	Industry	Services
Japan	1	26	73
India	24	28	48
Vietnam	22	40	38
Nepal	40	20	40
North Korea	30	34	36

Using **only** the information on China and Sources 1, 2, 3, 4 above and opposite, what **conclusions** can be drawn about the relationship between **China and her neighbours**?

You must **make** and **justify** a conclusion about **each** of the following headings.

• The urban/rural divide in China compared with some of her neighbours
• The relationship between the urban/rural divide and employment in agriculture
• The relationship between employment in services and their contribution to GDP
• The importance of China to the economies of the neighbouring countries

(Enquiry Skills, **8** marks)

[NOW GO TO QUESTION 4 ON PAGE 21]

[BLANK PAGE]

SYLLABUS AREA 4—INTERNATIONAL RELATIONS

QUESTION 4

(a)
> *In recent years some European countries and their allies have expanded their military actions beyond Europe.*

Explain, **in detail**, the reasons why *some European countries and their allies have expanded their military actions beyond Europe.*

In answering this question, you must refer to:

- A description of some of these actions.
- The reasons why such actions were taken.

Your answer **must** refer to recent examples you have studied.

(Knowledge & Understanding, **8** marks)

[Turn over

QUESTION 4 (CONTINUED)

(*b*)   Study Sources 1, 2, 3 and 4 below and opposite, then answer the question which follows.

THE GREAT EUROPEAN DEBATE

SOURCE 1

Membership of the European Union (EU)

1958   Belgium, France, W Germany, Luxembourg, Italy and the Netherlands
1973   Denmark, Ireland and the UK
1981   Greece
1986   Portugal and Spain
1995   Austria, Finland and Sweden
2004   Cyprus, the Czech Republic, Estonia, Hungary, Latvia, Lithuania, Malta, Poland, Slovakia and Slovenia.

For the future, Bulgaria, Croatia, Romania and Turkey still wish to join the EU.

Opinion Poll carried out in selected countries
Question: If the EU were scrapped, how would you feel?

	Unhappy (%)	Delighted (%)	Don't care (%)	Don't know (%)
Belgium	29	7	53	11
Finland	22	28	41	9
Germany	30	14	40	16
Ireland	44	3	34	19
UK	16	27	45	12
EU average	28	14	45	13

The 2004 elections for the European Parliament highlighted many issues of importance to the people of Europe. Just over 44% of the 350 million eligible voters in 25 member states cast their ballots, making this one of the biggest democratic exercises in the world.

Many pro-Europeans had great hopes for the new member countries in these elections but only 20% of the electorate in Poland voted, despite the huge amount of EU funding the country is likely to receive over the next few years. The Poles, along with the majority of EU voters, rejected the party in government, using this as a protest vote about domestic issues.

SOURCE 2: Percentage of votes gained by selected parties in UK elections for the European Parliament (1999 and 2004)

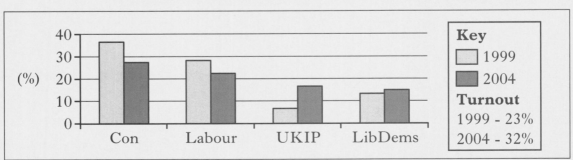

QUESTION 4 (b) (CONTINUED)

SOURCE 3:   Attitude of selected political parties towards the European Union

SOURCE 4: Results of an Opinion Poll

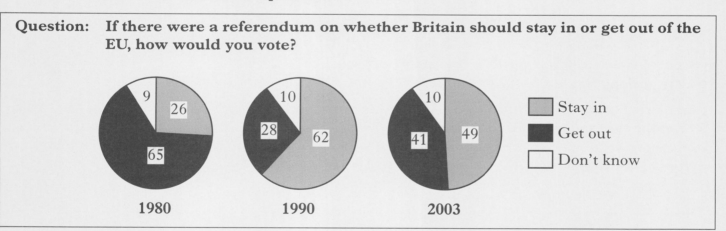

People in Britain and in other European countries no longer wish to be part of the European Union.

View of a UKIP voter

Using **only** sources 1, 2, 3 and 4 above and opposite, provide evidence **for** and **against** the view of the UKIP voter.

Overall, do you think the evidence **supports** the view? Give a reason for your answer.

(Enquiry Skills, **10** marks)

[END OF QUESTION PAPER]

[BLANK PAGE]

[BLANK PAGE]

G

2640/402

NATIONAL QUALIFICATIONS 2007	TUESDAY, 22 MAY 10.20 AM–11.50 AM	MODERN STUDIES STANDARD GRADE General Level

1   Read every question carefully.

2   Answer all questions as fully as you can.

3   If you cannot do a question, go on to the next one. Try again later.

4   In question 3, answer **one** section only; Section (A) The USA **or** Section (B) Russia **or** Section (C) China.

5   Write your answers in the answer book provided. Indicate clearly, in the left hand margin, the question and section of question being answered. Do not write in the right hand margin.

SYLLABUS AREA 1—LIVING IN A DEMOCRACY

QUESTION 1

(*a*)

Describe **two** ways in which supporters of a candidate can help during an election campaign.

To answer this question, you may wish to use the drawing above.

(Knowledge & Understanding, **4** marks)

QUESTION 1 (CONTINUED)

(b)   Study the information below, then answer the question which follows.

Political Participation by British voters

Survey Result

Question: Which of the following political activities have you been involved in?

Activity	2001	2005
Signing a petition	43%	60%
Contacting your councillor	46%	43%
Attending a meeting or rally	38%	43%
Contacting a local council official	64%	41%
Taking part in a demonstration or protest	9%	22%
Contacting a government official	24%	20%
Contacting your Member of Parliament	33%	28%

Write down **two** conclusions about changes in political participation in Britain.

You must **only** use the information above.

You should write **one** conclusion about **each** of the following.

• The change in the most popular political activity from 2001 to 2005

• The activity which has shown the least change in participation from 2001 to 2005

(Enquiry Skills, **4** marks)

[Turn over

QUESTION 1 (CONTINUED)

(*c*)

Shop Stewards help union members in a number of different ways.

Give **two** problems that a *Shop Steward might help their members* with.

For **one** of these problems, describe how the Shop Steward might help.

To answer this question, you may wish to use the drawing above.

(Knowledge and Understanding, **4** marks)

QUESTION 1 (CONTINUED)

(*d*) Study Sources 1 and 2 below, then answer the question which follows.

SOURCE 1

UK Trade Union Membership 2001–2005

Year	Men	Women	Total
2001	3,636,000	3,210,000	6,846,000
2002	3,532,000	3,308,000	6,840,000
2003	3,500,000	3,320,000	6,820,000
2004	3,432,000	3,353,000	6,785,000
2005	3,311,000	3,356,000	6,667,000

SOURCE 2

The Daily Herald

Report About Pay

In 2005, the average hourly pay for all workers was £10·21 compared to only £8·75 in 2001. Workers who belong to a trade union enjoyed a pay rate of £11·38 in 2005, whereas workers who were not members got an average of £9·72. There are still big differences in the rates of pay received by different groups of workers.

Workers benefit from being members of a trade union. Membership of trade unions continued to increase for some groups of workers.

View of Salma Khan

Using **only** Sources 1 and 2, give **two** reasons to **support** the view of Salma Khan.

(Enquiry Skills, **4** marks)

[Turn over

SYLLABUS AREA 2—CHANGING SOCIETY

QUESTION 2

(a)   Study the information below, then answer the question which follows.

Information on Millie Smith

Millie Smith is 72 years old and lives in a 4 bedroomed house which is too big for her. Her husband died recently and she feels lonely. She has always enjoyed having a garden. She has recently had a hip operation and finds it more difficult to move about or do the housework. Millie is starting to feel the cold more and more.

Millie wants to buy another house. She has seen the two houses below but is not sure whether **House A or House B** would **better meet her needs.**

House A — Ground Floor Flat

A ground floor, 2 bedroomed flat in a two-storey building with a shared central entrance.

There is double-glazing. Some more insulation and draught proofing is needed but this would be easy to do.

Elderly people live in the other 3 flats. All residents share a conservatory which looks onto a colourful garden.

House B — Bungalow

A one-storey, 2 bedroomed house. It would be straightforward to build a ramp and rails at the front to give easy access.

It has an overgrown garden, with many shrubs, that needs some work. There is a very pleasant garden summer-house for sitting in.

The bungalow is fully double glazed throughout and has full gas central heating. It is cheap to heat in the winter.

Using the information above, decide which house, **House A or House B**, would be the **better** choice for Millie Smith to **meet her needs**.

Give **two** reasons to **support** your decision.

You **must** link the information about Millie Smith to the house you have chosen.

(Enquiry Skills, **4** marks)

QUESTION 2 (CONTINUED)

(b)

> *Some elderly people are healthier than other elderly people.*

Give **two** reasons to explain why *some elderly people are healthier than other elderly people.*

(Knowledge & Understanding, **4** marks)

(c)

> *The government tries to help meet the needs of elderly people.*

Describe **two** ways in which *the government tries to help meet the needs of elderly people.*

To answer this question, you may wish to use the drawings above.

(Knowledge and Understanding, **4** marks)

[Turn over

QUESTION 2 (CONTINUED)

(*d*)   Study Sources 1 and 2 below, then answer the question which follows.

SOURCE 1

Scots spend too much time at work and work too hard!

Trade unions estimate that 16% of Scottish workers work more than 48 hours per week.   Investigations have shown that regularly working more than 48 hours a week increases the risk of illness.

A survey on holidays found some interesting results.   About 73% of Scottish workers said they often failed to take all their annual holidays.   37% of workers said they had been too busy to take their annual holidays, while 20% simply said that they had forgotten to take them.   50% also said that their annual holiday allowance of 20 to 25 days was not enough and should be increased.

SOURCE 2

Average weekly working hours for men	
Belgium	39·1
France	40·3
Greece	41·7
Italy	39·7
Portugal	42·1
Scotland	45·4
Sweden	40·2
EU Average	**41·3**

- Scottish men are the only men who work more than the EU weekly average.
- Working long hours can damage a worker's health.
- Very few Scottish workers fail to take all their annual holidays.
- Belgian men work the lowest number of hours.

Statements made by Sandy Brown

Using **only** Sources 1 and 2 above, write down **two** statements made by Sandy Brown which are **exaggerated**.

Using the information in the Sources, give **one** reason why **each** of the statements you have chosen is **exaggerated**.

(Enquiry Skills, **4** marks)

[Turn over for Question 3 on *Page ten*

SYLLABUS AREA 3—IDEOLOGIES

QUESTION 3

Answer **ONE** section only: Section (A)—The USA on pages *ten* and *eleven*

                    OR Section (B)—Russia on pages *twelve* and *thirteen*

                    OR Section (C)—China on pages *fourteen* and *fifteen*

(A) THE USA

(*a*)
> *People in the USA have many rights. They also have responsibilities that go with them.*

Describe **one** *right* that American people have.

Describe **one** *responsibility* that American people have.

In your answer you **must** use American examples.

(Knowledge & Understanding, **4** marks)

(*b*) Study the information below, then answer the question which follows.

The New York Herald

Bush wins again — 4 More Years

George Bush was returned to power for a second Presidential term in 2004.

Bush said to his opponents "To make this nation stronger and better, I will need your support and I will work to earn it." Bush told Kerry that he was "an admirable, worthy opponent."

Presidential Election Results (2004)

% vote for the candidates

1%
51%
48%

- ☐ Bush
- ☐ Kerry
- ☐ Others

Percentage of voters turning out to vote

1996	–	49·0%
2000	–	49·3%
2004	–	59·8%

In the 2004 Presidential election, the winner had a large majority. It also showed greater participation in politics by voters in the USA.

View of Eva Kaye

Using **only** the information above, give **one** reason to **support** and **one** reason to **oppose** the view of Eva Kaye.

(Enquiry Skills, **4** marks)

QUESTION 3 (A) (CONTINUED)

(c)

Give **two** reasons to explain why many American people have become rich and successful.

In your answer you **must** use American examples.

(Knowledge & Understanding, **4** marks)

(d) Study the information below, then answer the question which follows.

Opinion Poll — A Comparison

The percentage of American people who are supportive of President Bush's performance in selected policy areas

Policy Areas	2003	2004	2005
The economy	42%	46%	35%
Handling of the war in Iraq	52%	48%	32%
US campaign against terrorism	70%	57%	58%
Overall performance as President	**52%**	**47%**	**40%**

Statements made by Martin Baxter, an American journalist

- The lowest level of support for President Bush has always been in his campaign against terrorism.
- In 2005 less people approved of Bush's handling of the war in Iraq.
- Support for his handling of the economy has steadily fallen each year.
- The electorate's support for the President's overall performance has declined each year.

Using **only** the information above, write down **two** statements made by Martin Baxter which are **exaggerated**.

Using the information in the Opinion Poll, give **one** reason why **each** of the statements you have chosen is **exaggerated**.

(Enquiry Skills, **4** marks)

NOW GO TO QUESTION 4 ON PAGE SIXTEEN

QUESTION 3 (CONTINUED)

(B) **RUSSIA**

(a)

> *People in Russia have many rights. They also have responsibilities that go with them.*

Describe **one** *right* that Russian people have.

Describe **one** *responsibility* that Russian people have.

In your answer you **must** use Russian examples.

(Knowledge & Understanding, **4** marks)

(b) Study the information below, then answer the question which follows.

MOSCOW JOURNAL

Putin Wins Again

President Putin has been returned to power by the Russian electorate. This represents a terrific result for him. Russia now has a strong President for the next four years.

The result means that he now has the backing of the Russian people to get all his policies into law.

Presidential Election Results (2004)

% vote for the candidates

7%
4%
4%
14%
71%

- ■ Putin
- ▨ Kharitonov
- ▦ Glazyev
- ▩ Khalamada
- □ Others

Percentage of voters turning out to vote

1996	–	70%
2000	–	68%
2004	–	64%

In the 2004 Presidential election, the winner had a large majority. It also showed greater participation in politics by voters in Russia.

View of Maria Chakvetadze

Using **only** the information above, give **one** reason to **support** and **one** reason to **oppose** the view of Maria Chakvetadze.

(Enquiry Skills, **4** marks)

QUESTION 3 (B) (CONTINUED)

(c)

My father was poor. However, thanks to all that Russia now offers, I have become rich and successful.

Give **two** reasons to explain why many Russian people have become rich and successful.

In your answer you **must** use Russian examples.

(Knowledge & Understanding, **4** marks)

(d)   Study the information below, then answer the question which follows.

Opinion Poll — A Comparison

Question: How good a job is President Putin doing?

Comment	2000	2003	2005
Doing a good job	36%	42%	39%
Doing a fair job	20%	27%	32%
Doing a poor job	35%	27%	24%
Don't know	9%	4%	5%

Statements made by Alexia Gudrun, a Russian journalist

- More Russians thought Putin was "doing a good job" in 2005 than in previous years.
- In all three years, the majority of Russian people asked did not think he was "doing a fair job".
- In 2003, most Russians thought Putin was "doing a poor job".
- More Russians answered "Don't know" in 2000 than in other years.

Using **only** the information above, write down **two** statements made by Alexia Gudrun which are **exaggerated**.

Using the information in the Opinion Poll, give **one** reason why **each** of the statements you have chosen is **exaggerated**.

(Enquiry Skills, **4** marks)

NOW GO TO QUESTION 4 ON PAGE SIXTEEN

QUESTION 3 (CONTINUED)

(C) **CHINA**

(*a*)
> *People in China have many rights. They also have responsibilities that go with them.*

Describe **one** *right* that Chinese people have.

Describe **one** *responsibility* that Chinese people have.

In your answer you **must** use Chinese examples.

(Knowledge & Understanding, **4** marks)

(*b*) Study the information below, then answer the question which follows.

Duyun Times

Amy Li's Surprise Win!

Communist Party candidate, Amy Li, won a place on the Duyun People's Congress yesterday.

She was not expected to win. Long serving representative, Zhao Lung, was a surprise loser. Amy has promised to work hard to improve the lives of all local people.

Duyun Peoples' Congress Elections (2005)

% vote for the candidates

14%

40%

46%

- ■ Amy Li
- □ Zhao Lung
- ▨ Xi Phuz

Percentage of voters turning out to vote

1995	–	85%
2000	–	88%
2005	–	91%

In the 2005 election, the winner had a large majority. It also showed greater participation in politics by voters in Duyun.

View of Zi Yan

Using **only** the information above, give **one** reason to **support** and **one** reason to **oppose** the view of Zi Yan.

(Enquiry Skills, **4** marks)

QUESTION 3 (C) (CONTINUED)

(c)

> My father was poor. However, thanks to all that China now offers, I have become rich and successful.

Give **two** reasons to explain why many Chinese people have become rich and successful.

In your answer you **must** use Chinese examples.

(Knowledge & Understanding, **4** marks)

(d) Study the information below, then answer the question which follows.

China's Urban/Rural split

Year	Total population	Urban population	Rural population
1995	1·21 billion	30%	70%
2000	1·29 billion	36%	64%
2005	1·30 billion	41%	59%
2010 (estimate)	1·31 billion	44%	56%

Statements made by Lye Zhang, a Chinese journalist

- The Chinese population has grown since 1995.
- The urban population of China will double between 1995 and 2010.
- The biggest rise in the total population came between 2000 and 2005.
- The urban population has always been smaller than the rural population.

Using **only** the information above, write down **two** statements made by Lye Zhang which are **exaggerated**.

Using **only** the information in the table, give **one** reason why **each** of the statements you have chosen is **exaggerated**.

(Enquiry Skills, **4** marks)

NOW GO TO QUESTION 4 ON PAGE SIXTEEN

SYLLABUS AREA 4—INTERNATIONAL RELATIONS

QUESTION 4

(*a*)

> *Many different types of aid can help to meet the* **needs** *of some African countries.*

Describe **two** different types of aid which *help to meet the needs of some African countries.*

To answer this question, you may wish to use the drawing above.

(Knowledge & Understanding, **4** marks)

QUESTION 4 (CONTINUED)

(b)   Study Sources 1 and 2 below, then answer the question which follows.

<table>
<tr><th>SOURCE 1</th><th>SOURCE 2</th></tr>
<tr><td>NATO protects Afghans</td><td>Campaign proving difficult</td></tr>
<tr><td>Afghanistan is a poor country in Asia with Pakistan and Iran as neighbours. The mission by NATO forces in Afghanistan is the first they have undertaken outwith Europe.

They are there to help train, build up and support the Afghan army in the war against the Taliban. They are being successful in making the lives of the people better and more secure by fighting the Taliban. Some Afghans have had to flee from the fighting but they have been moved to clean, safe refugee camps.</td><td>NATO troops are involved in Afghanistan, a poor Asian country. Many local people have been forced to flee to refugee camps where the conditions are dangerous and filthy.

This is the first NATO campaign outside Europe and involves troops from many countries, including the United Kingdom. The campaign is very difficult with casualties mounting. The Taliban are proving hard to defeat as they are based in the mountains. Afghanistan is now suffering from lawlessness, misery and starvation.</td></tr>
</table>

Sources 1 and 2 give different views about **the involvement of NATO troops in Afghanistan**.

Write down **two** differences between these views.

You **must** only use information from the Sources above.

(Enquiry Skills, **4** marks)

[Turn over

QUESTION 4 (CONTINUED)

You are investigating the topic in the box below.

> **Scotland and the European Union (EU)**

Answer questions (*c*), (*d*) and (*e*) which follow.

(*c*)   As part of the **Planning Stage**, give **two** relevant **aims** for your investigation.

(Enquiry Skills, **2** marks)

You decide to send an e-mail to your MEP to discover more about the topic.

(*d*)   Give **two** advantages of sending an e-mail as a way of finding out information for your investigation.

(Enquiry Skills, **2** marks)

QUESTION 4 (CONTINUED)

Whilst researching your investigation you discover the following website.

Use the information below to answer question (*e*).

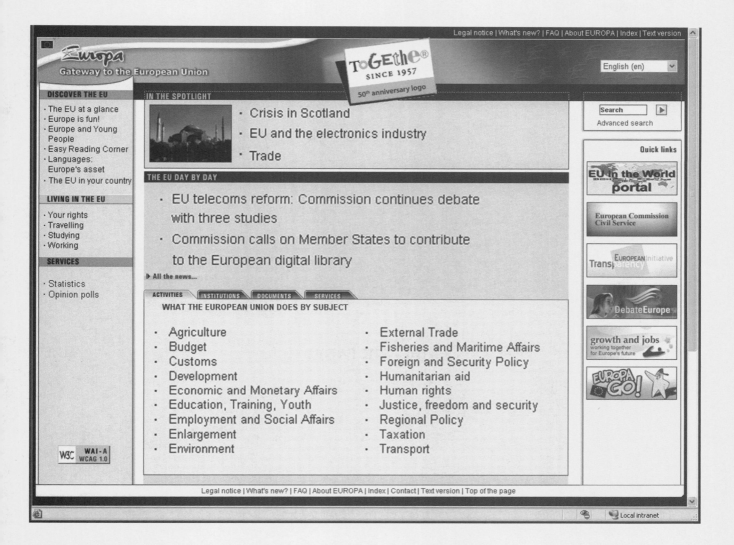

(*e*)   Give **two** ways you could use this website to find out more information for your investigation.

For **each** way, explain why it would be a **good** way to find out this information.

(Enquiry Skills, **4** marks)

[END OF QUESTION PAPER]

[BLANK PAGE]

[BLANK PAGE]

C

2640/403

NATIONAL
QUALIFICATIONS
2007

TUESDAY, 22 MAY
1.00 PM – 3.00 PM

MODERN STUDIES
STANDARD GRADE
Credit Level

1   Read every question carefully.

2   Answer all questions as fully as you can.

3   If you cannot do a question, go on to the next one. Try again later.

4   In question 3, answer **one** section only: Section (A) The USA **or** Section (B) Russia **or** Section (C) China.

5   Write your answers in the answer book provided. Indicate clearly, in the left hand margin, the question and section of question being answered. Do not write in the right hand margin.

[BLANK PAGE]

SYLLABUS AREA 1—LIVING IN A DEMOCRACY

QUESTION 1

(a)

> # The Daily Herald
>
> ## OPPOSITION GROWS TO NEW GOVERNMENT LAWS
>
> The Prime Minister has announced a package of new laws which he believes will improve the lives of the British people. They cover issues such as pensions, security and health. However, it is clear that many members of the public do not agree with these new laws and are ready to oppose the Government.

Describe, **in detail**, the rights that people have when opposing the introduction of new laws.

(Knowledge & Understanding, **4** marks)

(b)   Choose **one** of the following electoral systems.

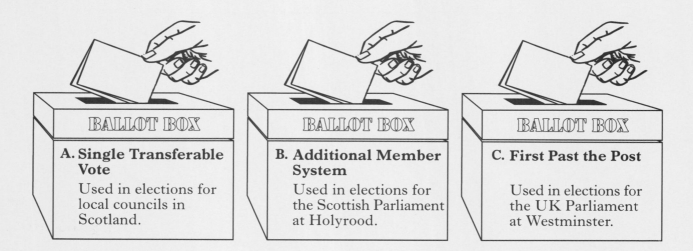

A. Single Transferable Vote

Used in elections for local councils in Scotland.

B. Additional Member System

Used in elections for the Scottish Parliament at Holyrood.

C. First Past the Post

Used in elections for the UK Parliament at Westminster.

Explain, **in detail,** the **advantages** of the electoral system you have chosen.

(Knowledge & Understanding, **6** marks)

[Turn over

QUESTION 1 (CONTINUED)

(c)   Study Sources 1, 2 and 3 below and opposite, then answer the question which follows.

SOURCE 1

UK General Election 2005: Selected Results

The UK RESULT			
Party	Vote (%)	MPs	Seats (%)
Cons	32	198	31
Labour	35	356	55
Lib Dem	22	62	10
SNP	2	6	1
Others	9	24	3

Scotland			
Party	Vote (%)	MPs	Seats (%)
Cons	16	1	2
Labour	39	41	69
Lib Dem	23	11	19
SNP	18	6	10
Others	4	0	0

Wales			
Party	Vote (%)	MPs	Seats (%)
Cons	21	3	8
Labour	43	29	72
Lib Dem	18	4	10
Plaid Cymru	13	3	8
Others	5	1	2

England			
Party	Vote (%)	MPs	Seats (%)
Cons	35·7	194	37
Labour	35·5	286	54
Lib Dem	22·9	47	8
Others	5·9	2	1

SOURCE 2

UK General Elections 1997 and 2005
Support for Selected Parties by Social class

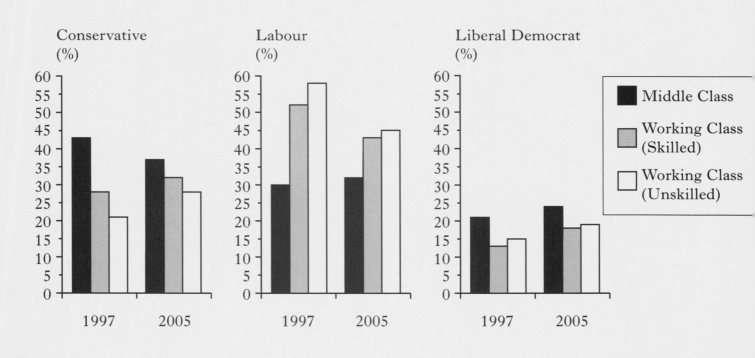

QUESTION 1 (*c*) (CONTINUED)

SOURCE 3

UK General Elections 1997 and 2005
Support for Selected Parties by Age Range

Age Range	Conservative 1997 %	Conservative 2005 %	Labour 1997 %	Labour 2005 %	Lib Dem 1997 %	Lib Dem 2005 %
18–24	25	24	50	42	17	26
25–34	27	24	50	42	17	26
35–64	31	33	43	38	18	22
65+	38	42	42	35	15	18

The Conservative Party did badly in all areas of the country. The Liberal Democrats, on the other hand, are the only party whose support increased amongst different age ranges and within different social classes compared with other parties, between 1997 and 2005.

View of Karen Mitchell

Using **only** Sources 1, 2 and 3, explain **the extent to which** Karen Mitchell could be accused of being **selective in the use of facts.**

(Enquiry Skills, **8** marks)

[Turn over

[BLANK PAGE]

SYLLABUS AREA 2—CHANGING SOCIETY

QUESTION 2

(a)

> *Some families are unable to meet the needs of their children.*

Explain, **in detail**, the reasons why *some families are unable to meet the needs of their children*.

(Knowledge and Understanding, **6** marks)

(b) Study the information below, then answer the question which follows.

Regional Unemployment in the UK (%)

Regions — North	1995	2005
Scotland	8·3	5·7
Northern Ireland	10·9	4·6
North East England	11·3	6·4
North West England	8·9	4·2
Yorkshire and Humber	8·6	5·0
West Midlands	8·9	4·3
Wales	8·8	4·4
Regions — South		
East Midlands	7·4	4·0
Eastern England	7·5	3·6
London	11·6	6·7
South East England	6·4	3·6
South West England	7·8	3·2
UK Average	**8·6**	**4·6**

> In 1995, unemployment was a bigger problem in the North than it was in the South. Ten years on, the situation was the complete opposite.

View of Tom Hicks

Give **one** reason to **support** and **one** reason to **oppose** the view of Tom Hicks.

(Enquiry Skills, **4** marks)

QUESTION 2 (CONTINUED)

(*c*) Study the information in the **"Focus on Families"** pamphlet below and opposite, then answer the question which follows.

Focus on Families

Introduction

Focus on Families looks at different types of families. Families in Britain have changed over the years.

Marriage and Divorce

More than 4 in 10 people over the age of 16 in the UK are married.

In 2005, the average age for first marriage was 31 for men and 29 for women. This had been 26 and 23 for men and women respectively 40 years earlier.

In 2005, the average age for divorce was 43 for men and 40 for women. This had been 39 and 37 for men and women respectively in 1995.

Marriages and Divorces in Britain

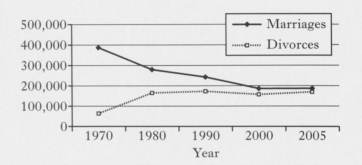

Family Structure

The total number of families reached 17 million in 2004. The "traditional" type of family has always been seen as a couple with dependent children. As the table shows, the percentage of families of each type in Britain has been changing. This may well have an impact on the welfare of dependent children.

People in each type of household (%)				
	1971	**1981**	**1991**	**2004**
One person	6	8	11	14
Families:				
Couple no children	19	20	23	25
Couple with dependent children	52	47	41	37
Couple with non-dependent children only	10	10	11	8
Lone parent family	4	6	10	12
Other households	9	9	4	4

QUESTION 2 (c) (CONTINUED)

Focus on Families (continued)

Lone Parent Families

% of families that are lone parent families (Scotland)

The main cities have a younger age structure than the overall population. As the map shows, there are wide variations in the distribution of lone parent families across Scotland.

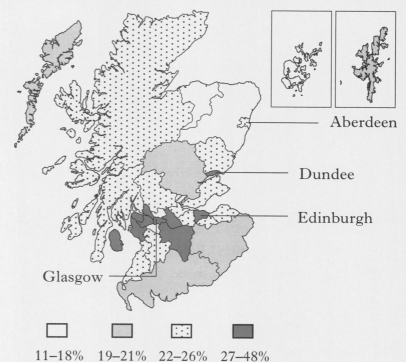

11–18% 19–21% 22–26% 27–48%

Families and Ethnicity

Some 9% of people in Britain are non-white. Ethnic groups differ in terms of family size and type.

62% of white families are married couples, 13% are cohabiting couples and 25% are lone parent families.

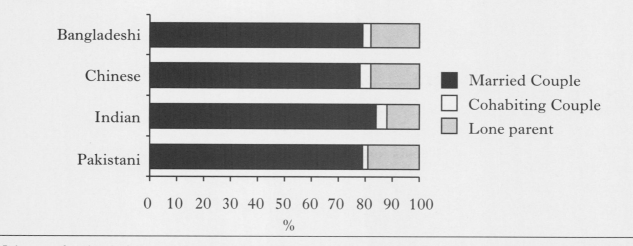

Using **only** the information from the "Focus on Families" pamphlet you must **make** and **justify** a conclusion about **all four** of the following headings.

- Changes in marriage and divorce in Britain.
- The link between changes in marriages and changes in the "traditional" family.
- The difference between the percentages of lone parent families in Britain and Scotland's four main cities.
- The main difference between ethnic minority families and white families.

(Enquiry Skills, **8** marks)

SYLLABUS AREA 3—IDEOLOGIES

QUESTION 3

Answer **one** section only: Section (A)—The USA on pages *ten* to *twelve*
           OR   Section (B)—Russia on pages *thirteen* to *fifteen*
           OR   Section (C)—China on pages *sixteen* to *eighteen*

(A) THE USA

(*a*)
> *Ethnic minority groups are now more likely to participate in politics in the USA.*

Explain, **in detail**, the reasons why *ethnic minority groups are now more likely to participate in politics in the USA*.

In your answer, you **must** use American examples.

(Knowledge and Understanding, **8** marks)

You have been asked to carry out **two** investigations.

The first investigation is on the topic in the box below.

> **Health care in the USA**

Now answer questions (*b*) and (*c*) which follow.

(*b*)   State a relevant **hypothesis** for your investigation.

(Enquiry Skills, **2** marks)

(*c*)   Give **two** relevant **aims** to help you prove or disprove your hypothesis.

(Enquiry Skills, **2** marks)

QUESTION 3 (A) (CONTINUED)

The second investigation is on the topic in the box below.

> **Education in the USA**

Now answer questions (*d*) and (*e*) which follow.

(*d*) While collecting information for your investigation you find out that your school has just started a twinning arrangement with a High School in the USA. You decide to **e-mail the Head Teacher** of the American school. You prepare the following e-mail. **Read it carefully**.

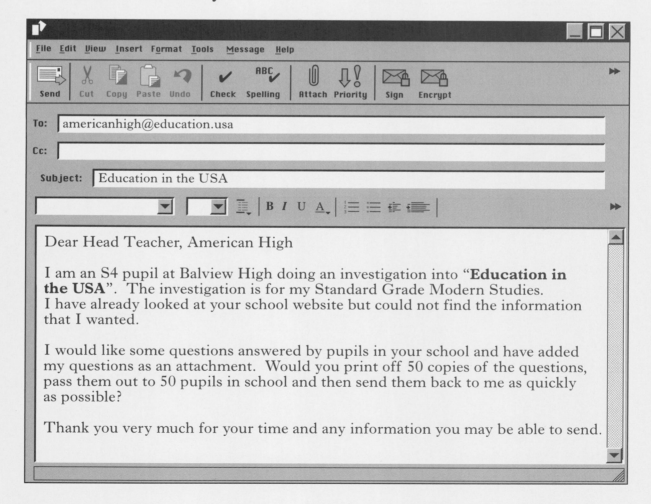

To: americanhigh@education.usa

Cc:

Subject: Education in the USA

Dear Head Teacher, American High

I am an S4 pupil at Balview High doing an investigation into "**Education in the USA**". The investigation is for my Standard Grade Modern Studies.
I have already looked at your school website but could not find the information that I wanted.

I would like some questions answered by pupils in your school and have added my questions as an attachment. Would you print off 50 copies of the questions, pass them out to 50 pupils in school and then send them back to me as quickly as possible?

Thank you very much for your time and any information you may be able to send.

Give **one good point** and **one bad point** about **the content of the e-mail** above.

(Enquiry Skills, **2** marks)

QUESTION 3 (A) (CONTINUED)

(*e*)   Here is a copy of the questions you wish to send. **Read them carefully.**

EDUCATION IN THE USA
INVESTIGATION QUESTIONS FOR STUDENTS

Where there is a choice please circle your answer.

Question 1
Which racial group do you belong to?

White   Black   Hispanic   Asian   Native American   Other

Question 2
How many students in your school wear school uniform?

All   More than half   Less than half   None

Question 3
Are your school meals good and do students get them free?

Yes   No   Don't know

Question 4
Why do Blacks and Hispanics not do well at your school?

_____

_____

_____

Question 5
In what ways do you think your school could be improved?

_____

_____

After checking the questions with your teacher, you are told that **two** of the questions are **poorly worded**.

Identify the **two** questions that are **poorly worded** and then explain, **in detail**, why each needs to be changed.

(Enquiry Skills, **4** marks)

[NOW GO TO QUESTION 4 ON PAGE 19]

QUESTION 3 (CONTINUED)

(B) **RUSSIA**

(a)

> *Many people in Russia like the fact that they can participate in politics.*

Explain, **in detail**, the reasons why Russian people *participate in politics*.

In your answer, you **must** use Russian examples.

(Knowledge and Understanding, **8** marks)

You have been asked to carry out **two** investigations.

The first investigation is on the topic in the box below.

Health care in Russia

Now answer questions (*b*) and (*c*) which follow.

(b) State a relevant **hypothesis** for your investigation.

(Enquiry Skills, **2** marks)

(c) Give **two** relevant **aims** to help you prove or disprove your hypothesis.

(Enquiry Skills, **2** marks)

[Turn over

QUESTION 3 (B) (CONTINUED)

The second investigation is on the topic in the box below.

Education in Russia

Now answer questions (*d*) and (*e*) which follow.

(*d*) While collecting information for your investigation you find out that your school has just started a twinning arrangement with a High School in Russia. You decide to **e-mail the Head Teacher** of the Russian school. You prepare the following e-mail. **Read it carefully**.

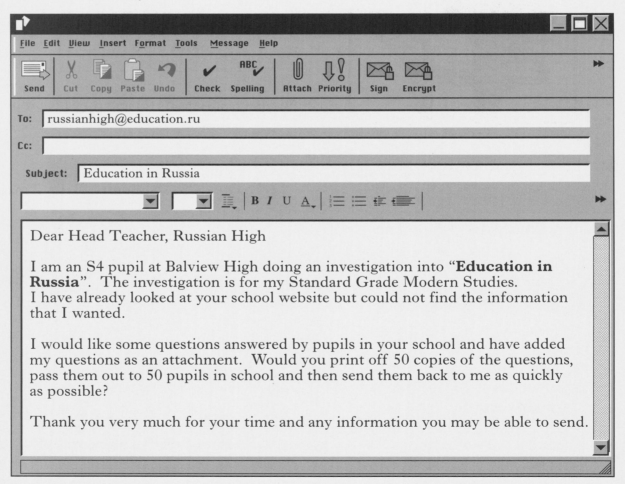

To: russianhigh@education.ru

Cc:

Subject: Education in Russia

Dear Head Teacher, Russian High

I am an S4 pupil at Balview High doing an investigation into "**Education in Russia**". The investigation is for my Standard Grade Modern Studies.
I have already looked at your school website but could not find the information that I wanted.

I would like some questions answered by pupils in your school and have added my questions as an attachment. Would you print off 50 copies of the questions, pass them out to 50 pupils in school and then send them back to me as quickly as possible?

Thank you very much for your time and any information you may be able to send.

Give **one good point** and **one bad point** about the **content of the e-mail** above.

(Enquiry Skills, **2** marks)

QUESTION 3 (B) (CONTINUED)

(*e*)   Here is a copy of the questions you wish to send. **Read them carefully.**

EDUCATION IN RUSSIA
INVESTIGATION QUESTIONS FOR STUDENTS

Where there is a choice please circle your answer.

Question 1
Which age group do you belong to?

11–12   13–14   15–16   17–18   Over 18

Question 2
How many students in your school wear school uniform?

All   More than half   Less than half   None

Question 3
Are your school meals good and do students get them free?

Yes   No   Don't know

Question 4
Why is it that girls always do better than boys at your school?

_____

_____

_____

Question 5
In what ways do you think your school could be improved?

_____

_____

After checking the questions with your teacher, you are told that **two** of the questions are **poorly worded**.

Identify the **two** questions that are **poorly worded** and then explain, **in detail**, why each needs to be changed.

(Enquiry Skills, **4** marks)

[NOW GO TO QUESTION 4 ON PAGE 19]

[Turn over

QUESTION 3 (CONTINUED)

(C) **CHINA**

(*a*)

> *Many Chinese people have difficulties participating fully in politics.*

Explain, **in detail**, the reasons why *many Chinese people have difficulties participating fully in politics.*

In your answer, you **must** use Chinese examples.

(Knowledge and Understanding, **8** marks)

You have been asked to carry out **two** investigations.

The first investigation is on the topic in the box below.

Health care in China

Now answer questions (*b*) and (*c*) which follow.

(*b*) State a relevant **hypothesis** for your investigation.

(Enquiry Skills, **2** marks)

(*c*) Give **two** relevant **aims** to help you prove or disprove your hypothesis.

(Enquiry Skills, **2** marks)

QUESTION 3 (C) (CONTINUED)

The second investigation is on the topic in the box below.

> **Education in China**

Now answer questions (*d*) and (*e*) which follow.

(*d*) While collecting information for your investigation you find out that your school has just started a twinning arrangement with a High School in China. You decide to **e-mail the Head Teacher** of the Chinese school. You prepare the following e-mail. **Read it carefully**.

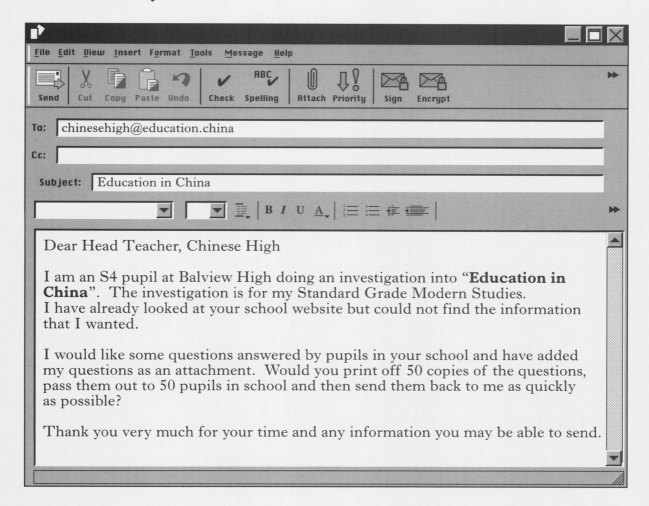

Give **one good point** and **one bad point** about the **content of the e-mail** above.

(Enquiry Skills, **2** marks)

QUESTION 3 (C) (CONTINUED)

(*e*)   Here is a copy of the questions you wish to send. **Read them carefully.**

EDUCATION IN CHINA
INVESTIGATION QUESTIONS FOR STUDENTS

Where there is a choice please circle your answer.

Question 1
Which ethnic group do you belong to?

Han   Zhuang   Uygur   Hui   Other

Question 2
How many students in your school wear school uniform?

All   More than half   Less than half   None

Question 3
Are your school meals good and do students get them free?

Yes   No   Don't know

Question 4
Why is it that children from rural areas always do worse at your school?

_____

_____

_____

Question 5
In what ways do you think your school could be improved?

_____

_____

After checking the questions with your teacher, you are told that **two** of the questions are **poorly worded**.

Identify the **two** questions that are **poorly worded** and then explain, **in detail**, why each needs to be changed.

(Enquiry Skills, **4** marks)

[NOW GO TO QUESTION 4 ON PAGE 19]

SYLLABUS AREA 4—INTERNATIONAL RELATIONS

QUESTION 4

(a) | *The policies of the European Union (EU) try to meet the **needs** of member countries and their citizens.*

Choose **two** of the following policies.

- Single European Currency (Euro)
- Enlarged Membership
- Common Fisheries Policy
- Aid to the Regions
- European Defence Force
- Common Agricultural Policy

For **each** policy, describe, **in detail**, the ways in which it tries *to meet the **needs** of member countries and their citizens.*

In your answer, you **must** use recent examples you have studied.

(Knowledge & Understanding, **8** marks)

[Turn over

QUESTION 4 (CONTINUED)

(b)   Study the article below and the information in the radio debate opposite, then answer the question which follows.

FOCUS ON CHAD

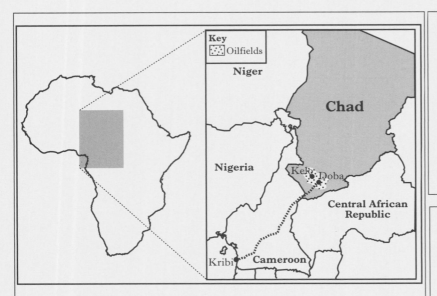

Introduction

Chad has many natural resources such as oil, uranium and gold which are under-developed. Only 200 sq km of farming land is currently irrigated and there are many natural hazards like drought. Lack of sanitation and clean water are major problems. The government is struggling to help its rapidly growing population.

Health Services

There is a lack of access to medical services. Many remote villages never see trained medical professionals and people cannot afford to travel to modern hospitals in the cities. They rely on local people who lack proper training. Doctors expect to be paid in advance by patients before treatment and there is a shortage of drugs.

Economy

Over 80% of the population rely on basic farming and livestock for survival. 75% of the population live on less than a dollar a day.

Few people are sufficiently qualified to leave the land to seek well-paid employment. 80% of the population live below the poverty line. Over $1 billion is owed in debt. The World Bank helped Western businesses to develop an oil pipeline from Chad to Cameroon.

People

Development Indicator	Chad	UK
Population	9·1 million	60·4 million
Population growth per year	3·0%	0·28%
Infant mortality per 1000 live births	94	5
Life expectancy	48 years	78 years
HIV/AIDS rate	5%	0·2%
Literacy rate	48%	99%

A conflict in Sudan has created a huge number of refugees which the government in Chad is trying to cope with.

Concerns of the people of Chad on selected issues

Question: What do you think is the most important issue facing Chad?

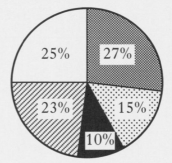

- Health
- Education
- Employment
- Access to fresh water
- Farming improvement

QUESTION 4 (*b*) (CONTINUED)

RADIO DEBATE

World Radio brings you a studio discussion about the best way to tackle poverty in Africa. Today's debate focuses on Chad.

What makes your project best for Chad?

Hello. I'm **Simon Rose** and I represent Rose Energy. We believe in supporting governments such as Chad's as they understand local conditions. Large-scale projects such as oil production are the best way to develop a country.

Good morning. My name is **Chrissie Smith** and I work for a non-governmental organisation called Helping Hands. We help local communities develop at their own pace. Small-scale projects provide a long-term solution.

What would be the main focus of your project?

We are prepared to invest $1 billion to create a second oil field in Chad. We will build a new road network in the south of the country, benefiting other industries. We hope to build a city hospital close to our proposed oilfield. Villages along the pipeline will have water pumps installed. 2% of our profits will go to the government as tax which could be spent repaying debts.

Helping Hands believes that health care and contraception are the key issues facing Chad. We will train local women to provide free community health care, reducing the spread of HIV/AIDS. Ten clinics across Chad will be set up, each costing $20 000.

What other issues do you believe are important for the development of Chad?

Without oil I see no future for the country. The economy currently relies on cotton and cattle. Jobs and improved services will only come with the development of the oil field and new infrastructure. Big schemes are best as the money spreads down through society.

The other key areas are farming and education. We must improve the income of farmers. This is a major obstacle to development. Also, very few children go to school as they are needed on the farm. It is crucial to begin teaching these children so they can be offered a better future. Small locally managed community projects are best suited to countries such as Chad.

Project One
Rose Energy

Project Two
Helping Hands

Which one of these projects is more suitable for Chad?

Using only **Focus on Chad** and the **radio debate**, explain which project, Rose Energy or Helping Hands, would be **more suitable** to help Chad develop.

Give **detailed reasons** to explain your choice and also why you **rejected** the other option.

In your answer you must **relate** the information about Chad to the information about the **two** projects.

(Enquiry Skills, **10** marks)

[END OF QUESTION PAPER]

[BLANK PAGE]

[BLANK PAGE]

G

2640/402

NATIONAL
QUALIFICATIONS
2008

THURSDAY, 22 MAY
10.20 AM–11.50 AM

MODERN STUDIES
STANDARD GRADE
General Level

1   Read every question carefully.

2   Answer all questions as fully as you can.

3   If you cannot do a question, go on to the next one. Try again later.

4   In question 3, answer **one** section only; Section (A) The USA **or** Section (B) Russia **or** Section (C) China.

5   Write your answers in the answer book provided. Indicate clearly, in the left hand margin, the question and section of question being answered. Do not write in the right hand margin.

SYLLABUS AREA 1—LIVING IN A DEMOCRACY

QUESTION 1

(a)

> *Members of pressure groups have rights and responsibilities.*

Describe one **right** and one **responsibility** that members of a pressure group have.

To answer this question, you may wish to use the drawing above.

(Knowledge & Understanding, **4** marks)

(b) Study Sources 1 and 2 below, then answer the question which follows.

<table>
<tr><td align="center">**SOURCE 1**</td><td align="center">**SOURCE 2**</td></tr>
<tr><td>

VIEW OF MALCOLM BROWN

There are about 5 million members of ethnic minority groups in Britain. The number of MPs from such ethnic groups rose slightly in 2005.

We do not need special arrangements to attract more women into Parliament. After the 2005 General Election, the number of women in the House of Commons rose to a historic high. 128 female MPs were elected. This shows that women are now well represented in the UK.

This was election win number three for Prime Minister Blair and his party.

</td><td>

VIEW OF JANE RENNIE

The 2005 election was the third win in a row for Tony Blair and the Labour Party.

With 128 MPs, there are more women in the House of Commons than ever before. However, with less than 20% of the total, women in the UK are still poorly represented when compared to other European countries. We must find new ways to encourage more women to become MPs.

The number of representatives from Britain's 5 million or so ethnic minority population has increased a little from 13 to 15 MPs.

</td></tr>
</table>

Sources 1 and 2 give different views about **representation in the House of Commons**.

Write down **two** differences between these views.

You **must** only use information from the Sources above.

Page two

(Enquiry Skills, **4** marks)

QUESTION 1 (CONTINUED)

You are investigating the topic in the box below.

CAMPAIGNING IN ELECTIONS

Answer questions (*c*), (*d*) and (*e*) which follow.

(*c*)   As part of the **Planning Stage**, give **two** relevant **aims** for your investigation.

(Enquiry Skills, **2** marks)

You decide to contact some political parties to help in your investigation.

(*d*)   Give **two** ways in which you could contact the political parties.

For **each** way you have chosen, explain why it is a **good** way to get information to help in your investigation.

(Enquiry Skills, **4** marks)

You decide to use your local library to help with your investigation.

(*e*)   Describe **one** way in which you could use your local library.

(Enquiry Skills, **2** marks)

[Turn over

SYLLABUS AREA 2—CHANGING SOCIETY

QUESTION 2

(a)

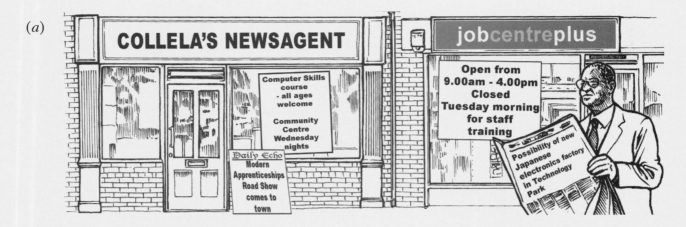

> *The Government tries to help unemployed people find jobs.*

Describe **two** ways in which *the Government tries to help unemployed people find jobs.*

To answer this question, you may wish to use the drawing above.

(Knowledge and Understanding, **4** marks)

QUESTION 2 (CONTINUED)

(b)

Technology has allowed many people to work from home.

Give **two** ways in which *technology has allowed many people to work from home*.

For **each** way, explain why it has allowed many people to work from home.

To answer this question, you may wish to use the drawing above.

(Knowledge and Understanding, **4** marks)

[Turn over

QUESTION 2 (CONTINUED)

(c)   Study the information below, then answer the question which follows.

Inverdee Council

Inverdee Council to spend £150,000 on new scheme.

Inverdee wants to meet the needs of young unemployed people in one of its most deprived areas. These young people need help with completing job application forms. They also need to improve their interview skills and ICT skills.

Inverdee Council is not sure whether **Scheme A** or **Scheme B** would **best meet the needs of young unemployed people.**

Scheme A	Scheme B
A Digital Community Centre	**Personal Advisors**

This scheme digitally connects 12 local community centres in Inverdee. It aims to give local unemployed people basic to advanced ICT training. Locals will have access to multi-media technology, including computers, scanners, digital cameras and data projectors.

The community centres will provide training, promote employment and assist in setting up new businesses.

The scheme would target a range of groups including young people. Help will also be given in completing application forms for anyone who feels they need it.

Job hunters in Inverdee are to get help finding work. A local voluntary organisation wants to deliver a new service to help young people communicate better with possible employers. It will concentrate on improving interview skills but also offer work experience.

The programme will be available to young people, aged 18 to 24, who are unemployed for six months or more. It will also give advice on filling in application forms for new jobs.

The scheme is confident it will make a real difference in getting young people into quality employment in Inverdee.

Using the information above, decide whether **Scheme A** or **Scheme B**, would be the **better** choice for Inverdee Council to **meet the needs** of young unemployed people.

Give **two** reasons to **support** your decision.

You **must** link the information about the needs of the young unemployed people to the scheme you have chosen.

(Enquiry Skills, **4** marks)

QUESTION 2 (CONTINUED)

(*d*)   Study the table below, then answer the question which follows.

Self-employment by ethnic group			
	2001	**2003**	**2005**
White	11·0%	11·9%	12·0%
Pakistani	21·8%	22·5%	21·0%
Indian	12·5%	13·1%	12·5%
Chinese	19·1%	18·3%	16·0%
Black Caribbean	7·1%	9·7%	8·0%
Black African	6·6%	6·2%	6·0%
Bangladeshi	12·3%	9·9%	14·0%

Self-employment amongst Whites and Bangladeshis has grown every year.
Pakistanis had the largest decrease in self-employment between 2003 and 2005

View of Abigail Smith

Using **only** the table above, give **two** reasons to **disagree** with the view of Abigail Smith.

(Enquiry Skills, **4** marks)

[Turn over

SYLLABUS AREA 3 — IDEOLOGIES

QUESTION 3

Answer **ONE** section only: Section (A)—The USA on pages *eight* to *eleven*

                                  OR Section (B)—Russia on pages *twelve* to *fifteen*

                                  OR Section (C)—China on pages *sixteen* to *nineteen*

(A) THE USA

(*a*)

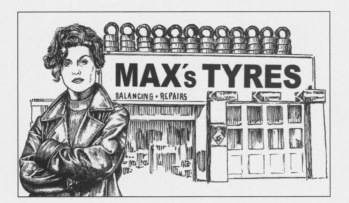 

MAX'S TYRES
Balance Sheet

Sales:	$550,000
Profit:	$240,000
Tax:	$ 25,000

Starting up a business can improve the lives of some Americans.

Describe **two** ways in which *starting up a business can improve the lives of some Americans.*

In your answer you **must** use American examples.

To answer this question, you may wish to use the drawings above.

(Knowledge & Understanding, **4** marks)

QUESTION 3 (A) (CONTINUED)

(b)   Study Sources 1 and 2 below, then answer the question which follows.

SOURCE 1

Information about selected countries		
Country	**Average Income ($)**	**Life Expectancy (Years)**
China	1,290	72
Japan	37,180	82
Russia	3,410	65
United Kingdom	33,940	79
United States	41,400	78

SOURCE 2

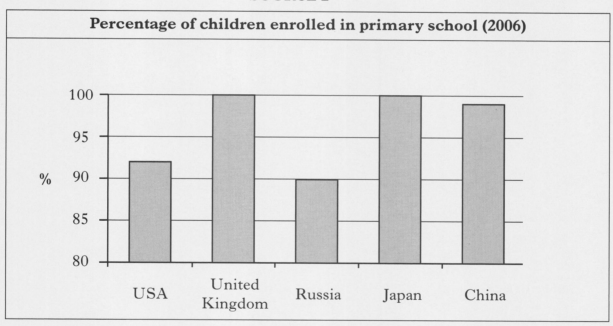

The USA enrolls less of its children in primary school than most other major countries. However, people in the USA have both the highest average income and live the longest.

View of Kelly Halcomb

Using **only** Source 1 and Source 2 above, give **one** reason to **support** and **one** reason to **oppose** the view of Kelly Halcomb.

(Enquiry Skills, **4** marks)

[Turn over

QUESTION 3 (A) (CONTINUED)

(c)   **ISSUES IN THE USA**

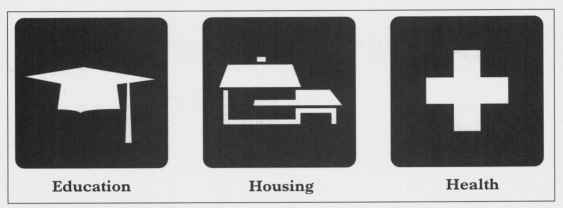

| Education | Housing | Health |

Some Americans are worse off than others.

Choose **one** of the issues from the box above.

For the issue you have chosen, give **two** reasons why *some Americans are worse off than others*.

In your answer you **must** use American examples.

(Knowledge & Understanding, **4** marks)

QUESTION 3 (A) (CONTINUED)

(d)   Study Sources 1 and 2 below, then answer the question which follows.

SOURCE 1

Hurricane Katrina hit the Gulf Coast of the United States on 29 August 2005, destroying towns in the states of Mississippi and Louisiana. It made one million people homeless, and killed almost 1,800 others. Americans were upset at the size of the disaster and how poorly prepared all levels of government were to deal with the problem. The President agreed that the government had been slow to respond. He promised "one of the largest re-building efforts the world has ever seen" to repair the damage.

SOURCE 2

Opinion Poll of American citizens

Question: **How well has the government done in re-building the Gulf Coast after Hurricane Katrina?**

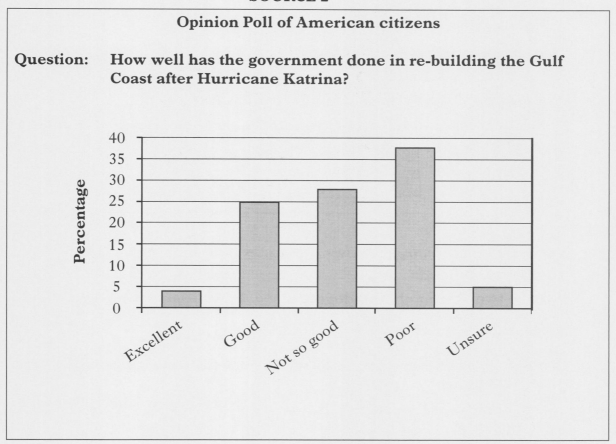

Hurricane Katrina caused a great deal of damage to the Gulf Coast area. However, the government was well equipped to respond to the disaster. President Bush has promised to re-build these states. The majority of people agree that the government is doing a good re-building job.

View of Reed Johnson

Using **only** Source 1 and Source 2 above, write down **two** statements made by Reed Johnson which are **exaggerated**.

Using the information in the Sources, give **one** reason why **each** of the statements you have chosen is **exaggerated**.

(Enquiry Skills, **4** marks)

NOW GO TO QUESTION 4 ON PAGE TWENTY

QUESTION 3 (CONTINUED)

(B) **RUSSIA**

(*a*)

> *Starting up a new business can improve the lives of some Russians.*

Describe **two** ways in which *starting up a business can improve the lives of some Russians.*

In your answer you **must** use Russian examples.

To answer this question, you may wish to use the drawings above.

(Knowledge & Understanding, **4** marks)

QUESTION 3 (B) (CONTINUED)

(b)   Study Sources 1 and 2 below, then answer the question which follows.

SOURCE 1

Information about selected countries		
Country	**Average Income ($)**	**Life Expectancy (Years)**
China	1,290	72
Japan	37,180	82
Russia	3,410	65
United Kingdom	33,940	79
United States	41,400	78

SOURCE 2

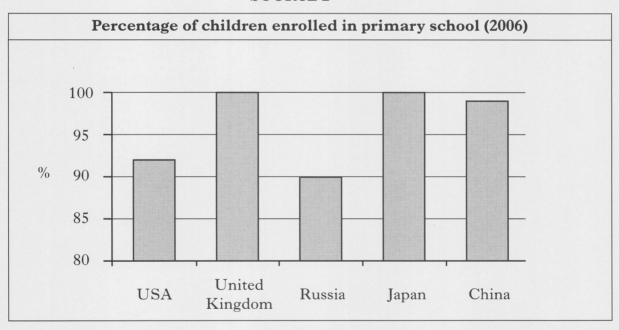

Russia enrolls less of its children in primary school than most other major countries. People in Russia also have both the lowest average income and shortest life expectancy.

View of Georgi Safin

Using **only** Source 1 and Source 2 above, give **one** reason to **support** and **one** reason to **oppose** the view of Georgi Safin.

(Enquiry Skills, **4** marks)

[Turn over

QUESTION 3 (B) (CONTINUED)

(c)

ISSUES IN RUSSIA

Education   Housing   Health

Some Russians are worse off than others.

Choose **one** of the issues from the box above.

For the issue you have chosen, give **two** reasons why *some Russians are worse off than others*.

In your answer you **must** use Russian examples.

(Knowledge & Understanding, **4** marks)

QUESTION 3 (B) (CONTINUED)

(*d*) Study Sources 1 and 2 below, then answer the question which follows.

SOURCE 1

The cost of living in Moscow has risen in the past ten years. Some tourists can spend as much as $390 a day whilst on holiday. Foreigners who live and work in Moscow admit a few items such as perfume can cost a little more than in their own country. However, shopping costs can be reduced by using shops on the outskirts of Moscow instead of the centre of the city. The majority of foreigners enjoy life in the Russian capital.

SOURCE 2

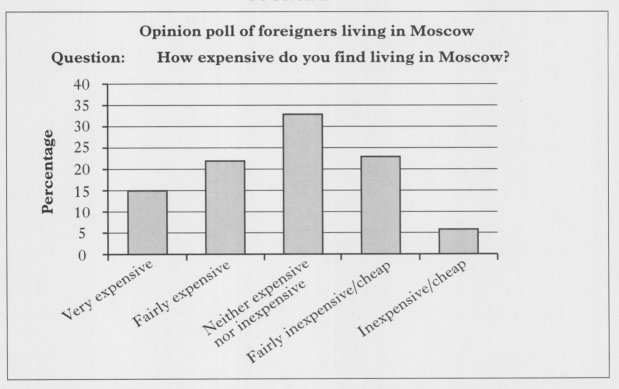

The cost of living continues to rise in Moscow. The majority of foreigners living in Moscow find the city expensive. Shopping costs are similar both in the centre and in the outskirts of Moscow. Foreign workers enjoy living and working in Moscow.

View of Maria Kirilenko

Using **only** Source 1 and Source 2 above, write down **two** statements made by Maria Kirilenko which are **exaggerated.**

Using the information in the Sources, give **one** reason why **each** of the statements you have chosen is **exaggerated**.

(Enquiry Skills, **4** marks)

NOW GO TO QUESTION 4 ON PAGE TWENTY

QUESTION 3 (CONTINUED)

(C) **CHINA**

(*a*)

> **CHOU'S TYRES**
> **Balance Sheet**
> Sales: 550,000 yuan
> Profit: 240,000 yuan
> Tax: 25,000 yuan

Starting up a business can improve the lives of some Chinese people.

Describe **two** ways in which *starting up a business can improve the lives of some Chinese people.*

In your answer you **must** use Chinese examples.

To answer this question, you may wish to use the drawings above.

(Knowledge & Understanding, **4** marks)

QUESTION 3 (C) (CONTINUED)

(*b*)   Study Sources 1 and 2 below, then answer the question which follows.

SOURCE 1

Information about selected countries		
Country	**Average Income ($)**	**Life Expectancy (Years)**
China	1,290	72
India	620	64
Russia	3,410	65
United Kingdom	33,940	79
United States	41,400	78

SOURCE 2

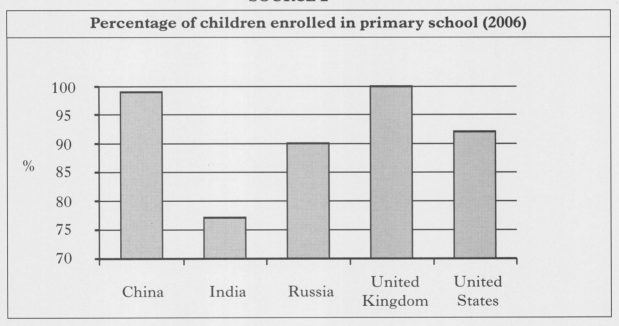

Percentage of children enrolled in primary school (2006)

China enrolls more of its children in primary school than most other major countries. People in China also have both the second lowest average income and shortest life expectancy.

View of An Qi

Using **only** Source 1 and Source 2 above, give **one** reason to **support** and **one** reason to **oppose** the view of An Qi.

(Enquiry Skills, **4** marks)

[Turn over

QUESTION 3 (C) (CONTINUED)

(*c*)   **ISSUES IN CHINA**

Education	Housing	Health

Some Chinese people are worse off than others.

Choose **one** of the issues from the box above.

For the issue you have chosen, give **two** reasons why *some Chinese people are worse off than others*.

In your answer you **must** use Chinese examples.

(Knowledge & Understanding, **4** marks)

QUESTION 3 (C) (CONTINUED)

(*d*)   Study Sources 1 and 2 below, then answer the question which follows.

SOURCE 1

2008 Olympics – China spends big!

China has spent almost $39bn on preparations for the 2008 Olympic Games. Most of the cash was spent improving Beijing's transport links, with 132 kilometres of new rail and underground lines built. Beijing has also modernised roads, power stations and water supplies. Those in the countryside around Beijing have not been so fortunate as sixty-nine villages have been demolished to make way for the new Olympic facilities. China hopes to be the centre of attention in 2008 and attract more investment.

SOURCE 2

Opinion Poll of Chinese citizens

Question: How happy are you that China has been awarded the 2008 Olympics?

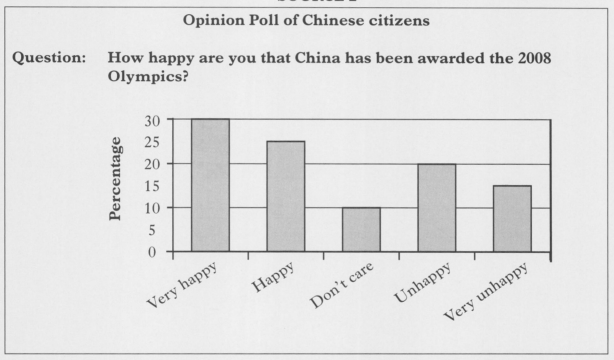

China has spent a lot of money preparing for the Olympics. The majority of Chinese people are not pleased about the Olympics coming to their country. However, everyone in the country should benefit from the Games. Beijing now has better transport links.

View of Zhan Zhenhua

Using **only** Source 1 and Source 2 above, write down **two** statements made by Zhan Zhenhua which are **exaggerated**.

Using the information in the Sources, give **one** reason why **each** of the statements you have chosen is **exaggerated**.

(Enquiry Skills, **4** marks)

NOW GO TO QUESTION 4 ON PAGE TWENTY

SYLLABUS AREA 4 - INTERNATIONAL RELATIONS

QUESTION 4

(a)

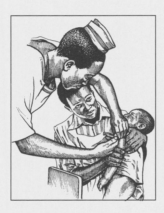

> *United Nations Agencies try to meet the needs of some people in less developed countries in Africa.*

Describe **two** ways in which *United Nations Agencies try to meet the needs of some people in less developed countries in Africa.*

To answer this question, you may wish to use the drawings above.

(Knowledge & Understanding, **4** marks)

QUESTION 4 (CONTINUED)

(b)   Study the information below, then answer the question which follows.

Data for selected NATO countries

Country	1990		2005	
	Numbers in Armed Forces ('000s)	Defence spending per person ($)	Numbers in Armed Forces ('000s)	Defence spending per person ($)
Greece	201	500	209	610
UK	308	770	216	530
USA	2,181	1,400	1,492	925
Turkey	769	110	816	115

Write down **two** conclusions about Armed Forces and Defence spending.

You should write **one** conclusion **with evidence** about **each** of the following.

•   The country with the biggest change in the numbers in its armed forces.

•   What happens to the numbers in the armed forces as defence spending rises.

You **must** only use the information above.

(Enquiry Skills, **4** marks)

[Turn over

QUESTION 4 (CONTINUED)

(c)

> ### 10 things you should know about the European Union (EU)
>
> 1. The European Union is a group of countries whose governments work together.
>
> 2. It's a bit like a club. To join you have to agree to follow the rules and in return you get certain benefits.
>
> 3. Each country has to pay money to be a member. They mostly do this through taxes.
>
> 4. The Single European Market has made trade between countries much easier.
>
> 5. There are 5 countries wishing to join at the moment.
>
> 6. 43% of all spending by the EU goes on Agriculture, Fisheries and helping the environment.
>
> 7. The EU has banned animal testing for cosmetics.
>
> 8. EU regional aid has raised living standards in poorer parts of Europe.
>
> 9. In 2006, 8 out of 10 EU citizens said they were fairly or very satisfied with living in the EU.
>
> 10. The EU has helped over 2 million young people study in another country.

> *Countries still wish to join the European Union.*

Give **two** reasons why *countries still wish to join the European Union*.

To answer this question, you may wish to use the information above.

(Knowledge & Understanding, **4** marks)

QUESTION 4 (CONTINUED)

(d)   Study the Timeline below, then answer the question which follows.

TIMELINE — NIGER FOOD CRISIS
KEY EVENTS 2004 – 2006

Date	Event
August 2004	Hardly any rain falls during what should be the rainy season. The crops which do grow are then eaten by several plagues of locusts.
November 2004	There are appeals for aid. Many people run out of food.
January 2005	Foodstocks are very low. There is very little food for people to buy. People march in the streets to draw attention to the problem.
July 2005	All Niger's debt is cancelled at the G8 summit. This should help greatly. Many children are dying of starvation.
August 2005	800,000 children under 5 are still going hungry. 40,000 tonnes of energy biscuits are sent to Niger by Italy.
September 2006	The rain fails to come again. A quarter of the population are reported to be hungry.

Niger has suffered greatly due to a lack of rain. People in Niger protested about the situation. No food aid was received by Niger. Debt is still a major problem for the government.

View of Lyz Graham

Using **only** the information above, write down **two** statements made by Lyz Graham which are **exaggerated**.

Using the Timeline, give **one** reason why **each** of the statements you have chosen is **exaggerated**.

(Enquiry Skills, **4** marks)

[END OF QUESTION PAPER]

[BLANK PAGE]

[BLANK PAGE]

C

2640/403

NATIONAL
QUALIFICATIONS
2008

THURSDAY, 22 MAY
1.00 PM – 3.00 PM

MODERN STUDIES
STANDARD GRADE
Credit Level

1   Read every question carefully.

2   Answer all questions as fully as you can.

3   If you cannot do a question, go on to the next one. Try again later.

4   In question 3, answer **one** section only: Section (A) The USA **or** Section (B) Russia **or** Section (C) China.

5   Write your answers in the answer book provided. Indicate clearly, in the left hand margin, the question and section of question being answered. Do not write in the right hand margin.

[BLANK PAGE]

SYLLABUS AREA 1—LIVING IN A DEMOCRACY

QUESTION 1

(a)

> *Trade union members have **rights during a dispute** with their employers.*

Describe, **in detail**, the **rights** trade union members have **during a dispute** with their employers.

(Knowledge & Understanding, **4** marks)

(b)

> *Women are better **represented** in the Scottish Parliament than they are at Westminster.*

Explain, **in detail**, the reasons why women are better **represented** in the Scottish Parliament than at Westminster.

(Knowledge & Understanding, **4** marks)

[Turn over

QUESTION 1 (CONTINUED)

(*c*) Study the Background Information about Gleninch and Sources 1 and 2 on the next page, then answer the question which follows.

BACKGROUND INFORMATION ABOUT GLENINCH CONSTITUENCY

- Gleninch is a constituency in the north of Scotland with a population of 35 265 people. It is a largely rural area with only one town, Inverinch, and a large number of scattered villages. The traditional industries of farming and fishing have been in decline in recent years. The unemployment rate is well above the national average.
- Many young people leave the area, moving to the big cities throughout the UK to look for jobs or to attend college or university.
- Tourism is very important to the local economy, with a lot of people employed in hotels, bed and breakfast accommodation and restaurants. Tourists tend to visit the area for a few days on short breaks, attracted by rare wildlife and spectacular, unspoilt scenery. However, there are a number of transport problems in the constituency, including high petrol prices and poor public transport.
- There is a proposal to build a wind farm in the area. This would involve the construction of 6 large wind turbines along the coast, as well as a 15-mile long power line built on tall pylons to take electricity to the rest of the country. This would create a few temporary construction jobs but will disturb local wildlife and impact on the scenery of the area.
- An American mining company wants to build a huge "super-quarry" into a mountainside near Gleninch. This will produce crushed rock to build roads, railways and houses throughout the UK. The new quarry will create 150 new jobs in Gleninch.
- At the last General Election, the constituency was won by the Labour Party with a majority of just over 1000 votes. The Liberal Democrats came second. They are convinced that, with the right candidate, they can win the seat at the next election.

A Statistical Profile of Gleninch Constituency (2006)

	Gleninch	Comparison with Scottish Average
Average Income	£21 185	−14%
Income Support claimants	15·1%	+22%
Unemployment Rate	5·6%	+13%
School leavers with no qualifications	3·6%	−33%
School leavers with Highers	58·6%	+13%
Serious Assaults	8·8 (per 10 000 people)	−73%
Housebreaking	3·8 (per 10 000 people)	−93%
Road Accidents	57 casualties	−44%

Survey of Local Liberal Democrat Members

Question: *How important are these issues to people in the area?*

Issue	Unimportant	Not Very Important	Fairly Important	Very Important
Environment	5%	25%	40%	30%
Health	2%	10%	53%	35%
Jobs	0%	0%	48%	52%
Women in Parliament	15%	52%	22%	11%

QUESTION 1 (c) (CONTINUED)

There are two people hoping to be selected by the Liberal Democratic Party to be the Party's candidate at the next General Election. Here are extracts from speeches they have made.

SOURCE 1

EXTRACT FROM CAMPAIGN SPEECH BY KIRSTY REID

- I support the proposed wind farm as it will provide many local jobs and help the local environment.
- Our local schools provide an excellent education. If selected, I will work to ensure this continues.
- Women make up over half the country's population and yet there are still very few of us who are MPs. This is a major priority for local party members and is an important reason why I should be the candidate.
- The local economy has been in decline recently. We need more jobs to keep our young people in the area. The new quarry will help with this, and I will work hard to see that it is allowed to go ahead.
- To attract more people to the area we need to improve transport links. I will make this a priority.

SOURCE 2

EXTRACT FROM CAMPAIGN SPEECH BY ROBBIE McKAY

- Tourism is very important to the area and so I will oppose the new wind farm as it will be an ugly blot on the landscape and deter tourists.
- Crime in Gleninch is among the worst in Scotland. I will campaign to improve policing in the area.
- Although new jobs are important, local Liberal Democrats are much more concerned about the environment. The new quarry will put more heavy lorries on our roads which are already more dangerous than the rest of the country. I will oppose it going ahead.
- The issue of health will be one of my main concerns, just as it is for local party members.
- Compared to the rest of the country, the people of Gleninch are not well-off. I will do all I can to improve this.

Use **only** the information about Gleninch on *Page four* and Sources 1 and 2 above.

(i) State **which person** would be the **more suitable** to be selected by the Liberal Democratic Party as their candidate for this constituency at the next General Election.

(ii) Give **three detailed reasons to support your choice**.

(iii) Give **two detailed** reasons why you **rejected** the other candidate.

In your answer, you **must relate** information about the constituency to the information about the **two** candidates.

(Enquiry Skills, **10** marks)

SYLLABUS AREA 2—CHANGING SOCIETY

QUESTION 2

(a)   **TYPES OF CARE FOR THE ELDERLY**

Community Care within their own home	Sheltered Housing	Residential Care Homes

Choose **one** type of care from the options above.

Explain, **in detail**, the ways in which this type of care **meets the needs** of some elderly people.

(Knowledge and Understanding, **8** marks)

QUESTION 2 (CONTINUED)

You have been asked to carry out an investigation on the topic in the box below.

> **Help for families in the UK**

Now answer questions (b), (c), (d) and (e) which follow.

(b)   State a relevant **hypothesis** for your investigation.

(Enquiry Skills, **2** marks)

(c)   Give **two** relevant **aims** to help you prove or disprove your hypothesis.

(Enquiry Skills, **2** marks)

Your Modern Studies class decides to use **Video Conferencing** to do an interview to help the pupils with their investigations into "**Help for families in the UK**".

Your teacher contacted your MP at Westminster, who said she would be willing to be interviewed. The interview set up is shown below.

| **Your MP in her office at Westminster** | **A secondary school classroom** |

(d)   Give **two relevant** questions which you could ask your MP to help with your investigation.

(Enquiry Skills, **4** marks)

[Turn over

QUESTION 2 (CONTINUED)

While collecting information for your investigation, you found the **Orinoco Web page** below which contained information about **Social Trends 2008**.

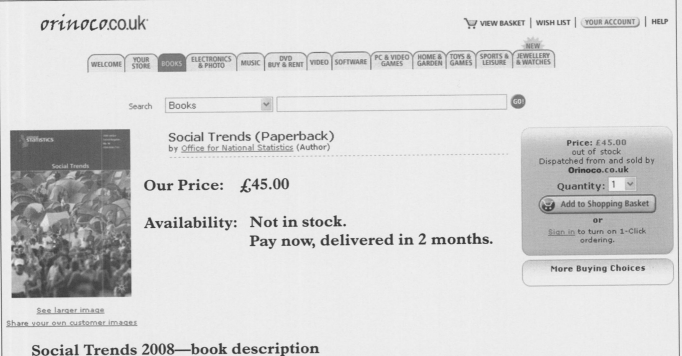

(e) Using **only** the Orinoco Web page, give one **disadvantage** of **buying** from this website and one **advantage** of **using** Social Trends 2008 in your investigation.

(Enquiry Skills, **2** marks)

[Turn over for Question 3 on *Page ten*

SYLLABUS AREA 3—IDEOLOGIES

QUESTION 3

Answer **one** section only: Section (A)—The USA on pages *ten* to *thirteen*
                                OR   Section (B)—Russia on pages *fourteen* to *seventeen*
                                OR   Section (C)—China on pages *eighteen* to *twenty-one*

(A) **THE USA**

(a) | *American citizens can* **participate** *in politics in many ways.* |

Describe, **in detail**, the ways in which *American citizens can* **participate** *in politics*.

In your answer, you **must** use American examples.

(Knowledge and Understanding, **8** marks)

QUESTION 3 (A) (CONTINUED)

(b)   Study Sources 1 and 2 below, then answer the question which follows.

SOURCE 1
Average Personal Income Level Per Person in the 10 Wealthiest US States ($)

	2003	2004	2005
Colorado	34 500	36 000	37 500
Connecticut	42 000	45 400	47 500
Delaware	34 100	35 900	37 100
Maryland	37 500	39 200	42 000
Massachusetts	39 500	41 800	43 700
Minnesota	34 000	35 900	37 300
New Hampshire	35 100	37 000	37 800
New Jersey	39 600	41 300	43 800
New York	36 100	38 200	40 100
Virginia	33 700	35 500	37 600

SOURCE 2
Income Distribution in the USA

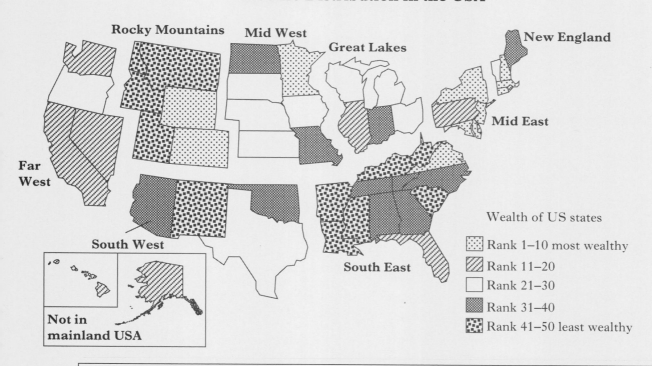

The biggest increase in personal income between 2003 and 2005 has been in Connecticut. The richest states in the US are all to be found in the Mid East of the country.

View of a Wall Street Economist

Using **only** the information above, give **one** reason to **support** and **one** reason to **oppose** the view of the Wall Street Economist.

(Enquiry Skills, **4** marks)

QUESTION 3 (A) (CONTINUED)

(c) Study the information in Sources 1, 2 and 3 below and on the next page, then answer the question which follows.

SOURCE 1

The Rockford Record

Your local voice, free to all 10 000 homes in Rockford City (23 May 2008)

New Housing Project Causes Local Anger

A recent public meeting in Rockford City Hall was attended by 500 local people. They were told about plans for a new gated community of 700 houses called "Red Pines". It is to be built by the Allan Building Company.

The gated community of Red Pines would be a walled housing development to which public access would be restricted. It would be guarded using CCTV and security personnel. The complex would have its own supermarkets, restaurants and bars.

The people at the meeting showed mixed feelings, for and against the possible development.

In 2004, gated communities housed 16 million Americans, about 6% of all households. Homeowners in gated communities live in upmarket and mostly white developments. Affluent black American homeowners are less likely than white people to live in gated communities.

The Red Pines Area Now

At the moment Red Pines is a beautiful wooded area. It is used by Rockford residents for walking and exercise. There is a jogging track, 3 football pitches and a rowing club on the river. Unfortunately, it floods occasionally as it is near to the river.

Doctor Joan Quincy said, "It is well known that Rockford residents are not very good at taking exercise. Health statistics show that compared to the rest of the USA we need to take more exercise. We need

Health and Exercise Statistics	Rockford	USA
Overweight	48%	35%
Bicycle riding	6%	16%
Exercise walking	16%	32%
Running/Jogging	4%	10%

the Red Pines area to keep our people healthy. We want to encourage more people to exercise in this area. Building houses would be a disaster for our community."

The building of Red Pines would also cause a great deal of disturbance in and around the town. There might be a few short-term benefits for the local community but long-term, there will be no real gain for the town as those living in Red Pines are unlikely to be spending much money in the shops in Rockford. They will get in their cars and drive to the city which is only 15 miles away.

Doctor Quincy is also Chairperson of the Rockford Residents' Association.

QUESTION 3 (A) (c) (CONTINUED)

SOURCE 2

What the people want

The Rockford Record decided to find out the views of local people about the "Red Pines" development. We conducted an opinion poll and received 8900 replies from 10 000 homes and feel that this survey shows the real views of the people.

The Questions: How Important	Unimportant	Not very important	Important	Very important
is it that Rockford stays a racially mixed town?	20%	15%	25%	40%
a problem is jobs to the people of Rockford?	15%	25%	20%	40%
is the Red Pines area for exercise?	20%	10%	45%	25%

Ethnic origin of Rockford's Residents

Other 8%
White 32%
Hispanic 29%
Black 31%

SOURCE 3

Leaflet from Allan Building Company

I am Chairman of the Allan Building Company and I was born in Rockford. I have stayed here all my life and want to do the best for Rockford. There is great demand for this type of housing from middle and upper income groups who would not live in Rockford because of their fear of rising crime there. We already have 500 new families from outwith Rockford, wanting to move into Red Pines whenever it is built. They are a mixture of young and old with an ethnic mix of 50% White, 25% Hispanic, 24% Black and 1% other groups.

Impact on Rockford

SHORT-TERM IMPACT	LONG-TERM IMPACT
• Skilled workers employed in the building of Red Pines. • Unskilled workers also needed. • Workers on-site spend money in local shops. • Building supply companies will increase trade.	• Unskilled jobs will be available, eg cleaners. • Jobs will be available in the new shops and restaurants. • Shops in Rockford will gain extra business from the new residents close-by. • Local shops have the opportunity to become suppliers to the new restaurants and bars which will open. • Flood prevention measures will stop flooding.

The Red Pines gated development will cause many problems for our health and change the ethnic mix of Rockford. It will bring few benefits to the people of Rockford.

View of Findlay Smith, Editor, The Rockford Record

Using **only** the information in Sources 1, 2 and 3, explain, **in detail**, **the extent to which** Findlay Smith could be accused of being **selective in the use of facts**.

(Enquiry Skills, **8** marks)

[NOW GO TO QUESTION 4 ON PAGE 22]

QUESTION 3 (CONTINUED)

(B)   **RUSSIA**

(*a*) | *Russian citizens can* **participate** *in politics in many ways.* |

Describe, **in detail**, the ways in which *Russian citizens can* **participate** *in politics.*

In your answer, you **must** use Russian examples.

(Knowledge and Understanding, **8** marks)

QUESTION 3 (B) (CONTINUED)

(b)   Study Sources 1 and 2 below, then answer the question which follows.

SOURCE 1
Index of growth of Industry and Agriculture in Russia

Sector	2001	2002	2003	2004	2005
Industry	1108	1443	1601	1681	2995
Agriculture	204	287	309	302	625

SOURCE 2
The ways in which the Russian people spend their money
(% of total)

	2002	2003	2004	2005
Foodstuffs	50·2	45·8	53·4	53·7
Alcohol	2·5	2·8	2·6	2·5
Non-foods	31·3	36·5	30·1	30·8
Services	16·0	14·9	13·9	13·0

Both Industry and Agriculture have grown each year between 2002 and 2005. The amount spent on foodstuffs is the only one which has seen a rise between 2002 and 2005.

View of a Russian Economist

Using **only** the information above, give **one** reason to **support** and **one** reason to **oppose** the view of the Russian Economist.

(Enquiry Skills, **4** marks)

[Turn over

QUESTION 3 (B) (CONTINUED)

(c)   Study the information from Sources 1, 2 and 3 below and on the next page, then answer the question which follows.

SOURCE 1

The Vorkuta Reporter

Your local voice, free to all 10 000 homes in Vorkuta (23 May 2008)

New Housing Project Causes Local Anger

A recent public meeting in Vorkuta Town Hall was attended by 500 local people. They were told about plans for a new gated community of 700 houses called "Sosny Woods". It is to be built by the Andropov Building Company.

The gated community of Sosny Woods would be a walled housing development to which public access would be restricted. It would be guarded using CCTV and security personnel. The complex would have its own supermarkets, restaurants and bars.

The people at the meeting showed mixed feelings, for and against the possible development.

Gated communities have been around for a long time in Russia. It used to be the case that they were only built for high-ranking political officials. This is changing and more and more are being built for Russians who are rich enough to be able to buy them.

The Sosny Woods Area Now

At the moment, the Sosny Woods area is a beautiful wooded area. It is used by Vorkuta residents for walking and exercise. There is a jogging track, 3 football pitches and a rowing club on the river. Unfortunately, it floods occasionally as it is near to the river.

Doctor Yuri Press said, "It is well known that Vorkuta residents are not very good at taking exercise. Health statistics show that compared to the rest of Russia we

Health and Exercise Statistics	Vorkuta	Russia
Overweight	48%	35%
Bicycle riding	6%	16%
Exercise walking	16%	32%
Running/Jogging	4%	10%

need to take more exercise. We need the Sosny Woods area to keep our people healthy. We want to encourage more people to exercise in this area. Building houses would be a disaster for our community."

The building of Sosny Woods would also cause a great deal of disturbance in and around the town. There might be a few short-term benefits for the local community but long-term, there will be no real gain for the town as those living in Sosny Woods are unlikely to be spending much money in the shops in Vorkuta. They will get in their cars and drive to the city which is only 15 miles away.

Doctor Press is also chairperson of the Vorkuta Residents' Association.

QUESTION 3 (B) (c) (CONTINUED)

SOURCE 2

What the people want

The Vorkuta Record decided to find out the views of local people about the "Sosny Woods" development. We conducted an opinion poll and received 8900 replies from 10 000 homes and feel that this survey shows the real views of the people.

The Questions: How Important	Unimportant	Not very important	Important	Very important
is it that Vorkuta keeps in-comers to a minimum?	20%	15%	25%	40%
a problem is jobs to the people of Vorkuta?	20%	40%	25%	15%
is the Sosny Woods area for exercise?	20%	10%	45%	25%

SOURCE 3

Leaflet from Andropov Building Company

I am Chairman of the Andropov Building Company and I was born in Vorkuta. I have stayed here all my life and want to do the best for the town. There is a great demand for this type of housing from middle and upper income groups. They are keen to move to Vorkuta because of their fear of rising crime in nearby cities. We already have 500 new families wanting to move into Sosny Woods whenever it is built. They are a mixture of age ranges and backgrounds. 73% are people with no connection to the town, 17% are people who live in nearby towns and 10% are Vorkuta residents.

Benefits to Vorkuta

SHORT-TERM IMPACT	LONG-TERM IMPACT
• Skilled workers employed in the building of Sosny Woods. • Unskilled workers also needed. • Workers on-site spend money in local shops. • Building supply companies will increase trade.	• Unskilled jobs will be available, eg cleaners. • Jobs will be available in the new shops and restaurants. • Shops in Vorkuta will gain extra business from the new residents close-by. • Local shops have the opportunity to become suppliers to the new restaurants and bars which will open. • Flood prevention measures will stop flooding.

The Sosny Woods Gated Development will cause many problems for our health and allow outsiders to dominate Vorkuta. It will bring few benefits to the people of Vorkuta.

View of Dmitri Arshavin, Editor, The Vorkuta Reporter

Using **only** the information in Sources 1, 2 and 3, explain, **in detail**, **the extent to which** Dmitri Arshavin could be accused of being **selective in the use of facts**.

(Enquiry Skills, **8** marks)

[NOW GO TO QUESTION 4 ON PAGE 22]

QUESTION 3 (CONTINUED)

(C) **CHINA**

(a) | *Chinese citizens can **participate** in politics in many ways.* |

Describe, **in detail**, the ways in which *Chinese citizens can **participate** in politics.*

In your answer, you **must** use Chinese examples.

(Knowledge and Understanding, **8** marks)

QUESTION 3 (C) (CONTINUED)

(b)   Study Sources 1 and 2 below, then answer the question which follows.

SOURCE 1
Average Personal Income
Top Ten Chinese Regions (Yuan)

Region	2003	2004	2005
Beijing	35 000	37 000	39 500
Tianjin	29 500	31 500	34 000
Hebei	13 000	13 500	13 500
Liaoning	15 000	16 500	17 000
Heilongjiang	13 000	14 000	15 500
Shanghai	51 000	55 500	61 000
Zhejiang	21 000	24 000	25 000
Fujian	15 500	17 000	18 000
Shangdong	16 000	17 000	17 500
Guangdong	18 500	20 000	21 000

SOURCE 2
China's Ten Richest Regions

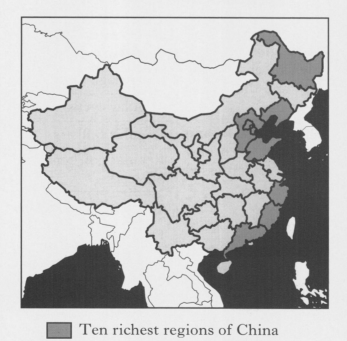

☐ Ten richest regions of China
☐ Rest of China

> The greatest increase in personal income has been experienced by those living in Shanghai. However, the wealthiest regions are evenly distributed throughout China.

View of Chinese Economist

Using **only** the information above, give **one** reason to **support** and **one** reason to **oppose** the view of the Chinese Economist.

(Enquiry Skills, **4** marks)

QUESTION 3 (C) (CONTINUED)

(c) Study the information from Sources 1, 2 and 3 below and on the next page, then answer the question which follows.

SOURCE 1

The Hankou Herald

Free to all 50 000 residents. Published by the Peoples' Congress of Hankou.

Joy as riverside housing is opened

The city authorities announced yesterday that the brand new "Riverside Garden" development of top quality houses is to open next month. The development (next to the Anze river) attracted 300 building jobs to the area, which have benefited Hankou's economy.

The new housing is known as a "Gated Community". This means that a wall will surround the 500 houses and local people will be employed as security guards and CCTV operators. Around 300 local people will have well-paid jobs in the community's facilities, eg medical centre, golf course, tennis courts, shops and gym.

The housing is very high quality and will attract many of the region's most successful business people who are looking for an escape from the city, and the chance to relax, play sport and socialise.

It will raise the profile of the area and possibly tempt more people to open new businesses in Hankou which is depressed economically and in need of a boost.

The Riverside area before

The area was only used by a few fishermen. Wages were poor and it was the only work available.

The town's people rarely went there. Sports facilities in all parts of the town, including the Riverside area, were very poor.

Local doctor speaks out

Dr Pu Zihao says, "It is well known that Hankou residents are not very good at taking exercise. Health statistics show that compared to the rest of China we need to be more active. We need new sporting facilities in the Riverside area to keep our people healthy. Building these houses is good for our community".

"Anyone will be able to use the sports facilities if they are willing to pay the yearly Sports Club membership fee of only 50 yuan."

(Dr Pu is a member of the "Healthy Hankou Campaign".)

Health and Exercise Statistics	Hankou	China
Overweight	27%	21%
Regular cyclists	64%	73%
Regular walkers	51%	78%
Regular golf/tennis players	1%	8%

An economic boost!

The people of Hankou have tried for many years to lift themselves out of poverty but they have not succeeded. Average wages are lower than the Chinese average and have shown little improvement in the last few years.

Average Wages (yuan)

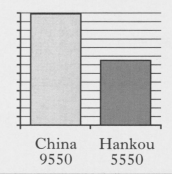

China 9550   Hankou 5550

QUESTION 3 (C) (c) (CONTINUED)

SOURCE 2

What the people want

We decided to find out the views of the local people about the Riverside development. We sent questionnaires to 10 000 local homes and received 8900 replies. The views of local people really have been heard.

Question: How important are the following things for Hankou?

	Unimportant	Not very important	Important	Very important
Higher pay	13%	13%	20%	54%
Attracting new businesses	5%	14%	30%	51%
Protecting existing farmers and fishermen	40%	25%	26%	9%

View of Li Jie – a local fisherman

I have lost my job and so have six of my friends. Hankou fishermen are all against this new housing development. Riverside Garden might bring a few short-term benefits for the local community but, in the long term, there will be no real gain for the town. Those living in Riverside Garden are unlikely to be spending much money in the shops in Hankou. They will only use the shops in Riverside Garden as there will be little to interest them in Hankou or they will get in their cars and drive to the city which is only one hour's drive away.

SOURCE 3

Leaflet from Hankou Authorities

IMPACT ON HANKOU

- Unskilled jobs will be available, eg cleaners.
- Jobs will be available in the new shops and restaurants.
- Shops in Hankou will gain extra business from the new residents close-by.
- Local shops have the opportunity to become suppliers to the new restaurants and bars which will open.
- Affordable sports facilities

The Riverside Gated Development will improve the health of people living in Hankou. It will bring much needed benefits to the people of Hankou. Everyone living in Hankou is excited by the opening of Riverside Garden.

View of Pu Wei, Editor, The Hankou Herald

Using **only** the information in Sources 1, 2 and 3, explain, **in detail**, **the extent to which** Pu Wei could be accused of being **selective in the use of facts**.

(Enquiry Skills, **8** marks)

[NOW GO TO QUESTION 4 ON PAGE 22]

SYLLABUS AREA 4—INTERNATIONAL RELATIONS

QUESTION 4

(a)   **SELECTED ISSUES IN AFRICA**

HIV/AIDS on the increase in large parts of Africa	Civil wars rage on in parts of Africa	Prices fall on a number of raw materials produced in some African countries

Choose **one** issue from the boxes above.

Explain, **in detail**, why your chosen issue may prevent some African governments **meeting the needs** of their people.

(Knowledge & Understanding, **4** marks)

QUESTION 4 (CONTINUED)

(b)

> *European governments have taken actions to protect their populations from possible threats to their security.*

Describe, **in detail**, some of the actions taken by *European governments to protect their populations from possible threats to their security.*

(Knowledge & Understanding, **4** marks)

[Turn over

QUESTION 4 (CONTINUED)

(*c*)   Study the information in Sources 1, 2 and 3 below and on the next page, then answer the question which follows.

SOURCE 1
Millennium Development Goals

The Millennium Development Goals were agreed by 189 countries in New York in 2000.

Selected Millennium Development Goals

1:    **Reduce child mortality**

2:    **Achieve primary education for all**

3:    **Remove extreme poverty and hunger**

4:    **Combat diseases**

These goals represented a commitment by rich and poor nations to expand social and economic progress in all regions of the world, as well as creating a global partnership for reducing levels of poverty and suffering in less developed countries by 2015.

Many are now questioning the commitment of the More Developed Countries to making these goals a reality as few MDCs give the UN recommended 0·7% of Gross National Income (GNI).

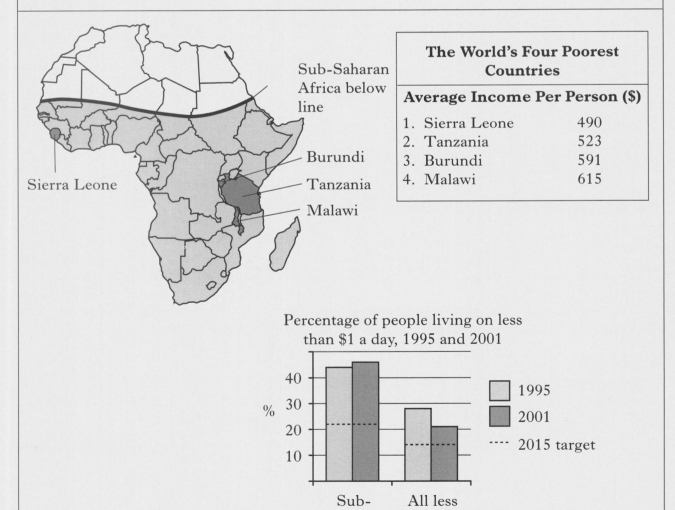

The World's Four Poorest Countries

Average Income Per Person ($)	
1. Sierra Leone	490
2. Tanzania	523
3. Burundi	591
4. Malawi	615

Percentage of people living on less than $1 a day, 1995 and 2001

QUESTION 4 (c) (CONTINUED)

SOURCE 2: Aid given by selected Donor Countries

Selected Donor Countries	Aid Given			Largest recipients ($ millions)
	2004 $ billions (% of GNI)	2010 (prediction) $ billions (% of GNI)	% increase	
UK	7·88 (0·36)	14·60 (0·59)	85	1. India ($419) 2. Bangladesh ($267) 3. Tanzania ($265)
USA	19·7 (0·17)	24·00 (0·18)	22	1. Iraq ($2286) 2. Congo ($804) 3. Egypt ($767)
Portugal	1·03 (0·63)	0·93 (0·51)	−10	1. Angola ($367) 2. Cape Verde ($39) 3. Timor ($34)
Italy	2·46 (0·15)	9·26 (0·51)	276	1. Dem. Rep. Congo ($235) 2. China ($52) 3. Tunisia ($41)

SOURCE 3

Four Poorest African Countries – Progress on selected Millennium Development Goals								
	Sierra Leone		Tanzania		Burundi		Malawi	
Selected Indicators Year	1996	2006	1996	2006	1996	2006	1996	2006
% of population undernourished	44	50	50	44	63	67	50	34
Child Mortality (per 1000 births)	293	283	159	126	190	190	216	175
% 1 year olds vaccinated against measles	37	64	49	91	80	75	90	80
% Primary school enrolment	43	73	94	95	43	57	48	98

Using **only** the information above and opposite, you must **make** and **justify** conclusions about progress towards the Millennium Development Goals using the **four** headings below.

- Progress towards Millennium Development Goal 1
- Progress towards **all** of Millennium Development Goal 3
- The commitment of More Developed Countries to meeting the UN aid recommendation
- The commitment of Donor Countries to the world's **four poorest** nations

(Enquiry Skills, **8** marks)

[END OF QUESTION PAPER]

[BLANK PAGE]

[BLANK PAGE]

[BLANK PAGE]

[BLANK PAGE]

[BLANK PAGE]

[BLANK PAGE]

[BLANK PAGE]

[BLANK PAGE]

Acknowledgements

Leckie & Leckie is grateful to the copyright holders, as credited, for permission to use their material:

The following companies have very generously given permission to reproduce their copyright material free of charge:
Unicef for their logo (2004 General paper p 13 and 2006 General p 15); Who for their logo (2004 General paper p 13);
ICM Research for the table 'Support for Selected Political Parties in Opinion Polls' (2004 General paper p 3);
HMSO for a table © Crown Copyright (2006 Credit Paper p 3);
HMSO for 3 logos © Crown Copyright (2006 Credit Paper p 4)
Scottish Enterprise National for the logos for Skillseekers and Modern Apprenticeships (2006 Credit p 4);
The Labour Party for use of their logo (2006 Credit paper p 23);
The Conservative Party for use of their logo (2006 Credit paper p 23).